ULTIMATE
ROAD TRIP

12 JOURNEYS
that shape your future

Jay Stewart

DESTINY IMAGE® PUBLISHERS, INC.

P.O. Box 310, Shippensburg, PA 17257-0310

"Speaking to the Purposes of God for This Generation and for the Generations to Come."

This book and all other Destiny Image, Revival Press, MercyPlace, Fresh Bread, Destiny Image Fiction, and Treasure House books are available at Christian bookstores and distributors worldwide.

For a U.S. bookstore nearest you, call **1-800-722-6774**.

For more information on foreign distributors, call **717-532-3040**.

Reach us on the Internet: **www.destinyimage.com**.

Trade Paper ISBN 13: 978-0-7684-3217-6

Hardcover ISBN 13: 978-0-7684-3393-7

Larg Print ISBN 13: 978-0-7684-3394-4

Ebook ISBN 13: 978-0-7684-9124-1

For Worldwide Distribution, Printed in the U.S.A.

1 2 3 4 5 6 7 8 9 / 14 13 12 11 10 9

Dedication

THIS book is dedicated to my wife, Melanie, who has faithfully journeyed with me for nearly three decades. She has been a rock through some very thrilling and many nerve-racking adventures of life, including cultivating a ministry, planting and growing a church, and raising four children. I would also like to dedicate this book to close family and friends who have remained so faithful to me throughout the journeys of life. And last, but certainly not least, this book is dedicated to the people who make up the community of believers known as The Refuge. Being on this journey with you is more thrilling than skydiving!

Acknowledgments

I would like to thank Nina Gass for her assistance in writing and for her sharp editorial skills.

I would also like to thank my amazing staff at The Refuge for their input and contributions to this endeavor, as well as for the way they are walking out their journeys of life with such courage and excellence.

Endorsements

Ultimate Road Trip—12 Journeys That Shape Your Future is a literary GPS designed to assist you in navigating your way to purpose and joy. Reflecting on true stories of the *journey's* of others and the Word of God, Jay Stewart's insight and creativity are refreshing and compelling. Everyone from business leaders, to stay-at-home moms, to students and church leaders will receive valuable tools for everyday victory. I highly recommend this great work!

—Jack W. Hayford
Chancellor, The King's Seminary
Founding Pastor, The Church on the Way

Over the past ten years I've been so privileged to call this anointed man of God my pastor and close friend. He's walked beside me in the greatest and darkest parts of my personal "road trip" in the Lord. The pages of this book contain life-giving words that are backed up by a life lived truly in pursuit of Jesus. Here's to the journey!

—Mike Weaver
Singer/Songwriter, Big Daddy Weave

Many people are on life's journey with no idea where they're going. If they're not careful, they may end up nowhere! With insight that is both engaging and practical, Jay Stewart comes alongside to help us find our way. This is a book that will speak to a new Christian and a mature believer. I wholeheartedly recommend it!

—Robert Whitlow
Best-selling author of *Higher Hope*

Knowing your destination and charting a course for the journey are keys to walking in the power of God's purposes. In this book, Jay Stewart has strategically captured vital principles that will help you move forward in your calling in God. The practical wisdom and creative exploration of the many aspects of life's journey will connect you to the Lord's path that brings triumph and victory.

—Dr. Robert Stearns
Executive Director, Eagles' Wings Ministries
Clarence, New York

I commend Pastor Jay Stewart for this wonderful work. Many pastors are quick to furnish a theological rendition of the Gospel, which Jay is quite able to do. However, we need to transform the theology of the Bible into practical steps that can be applied to our lives, and Jay has done this masterfully. His insights in this book are filled with wisdom and instruction, and I believe it should be in every believer's library. In these confusing times, we need a spiritual compass to guide us through difficulties that we face. *Ultimate Road Trip* will serve to assist you in the decision-making processes of your life.

—Bishop Paul D. Zink
Senior Pastor, New Life Christian Fellowship
Jacksonville, Florida

Jay Stewart is a faithful shepherd of the flock and a reliable guide for the journey of life. His new book is chock full of practical insights that will help you flourish on your own journey in God—and finish strong in the end.

—Dr. Michael L. Brown, President
FIRE School of Ministry
Concord, North Carolina

Contents

Introduction

*It is good to have an end to journey towards, but
it is the journey that matters in the end.*
—Ursula K. LeGuinn

A S a young boy, trips in the car with the family were exciting adventures that often led to unfamiliar places and great memories in spite of the mishaps. I am sure that you have some stories to tell as well. Mine is about the time my brother threw up in the back seat and the car smelled like vomit for the rest of the vacation. As an adult, I still love to travel. I have had the privilege of seeing much of the United States as well as numerous countries on four other continents. As fun and exciting as traveling can be, it does have its negatives, such as security lines at the airport, fees for checked bags, crowded interstates, car trouble, blow-outs, lost luggage, and Montezuma's Revenge!

No matter what happens to us, we can, no doubt, agree that life is an interesting, intriguing, and challenging journey. Learning to navigate through the challenges and storms of life can be tricky. A journey has its ups and downs, breakthroughs and impasses, wins and losses. We tend to feel drawn to journeys because they seem to involve a definite beginning and, usually, some sort of resolution. In between, there can be varying degrees of drama, romance, intrigue, and excitement.

Many read books about other people's lives because we are fascinated with how other's have experienced—and are experiencing—their journey through life. We are drawn to explorers, people who went from rags to riches, and those who have overcome enormous obstacles to regain their health and happiness. The reason that we are attracted to stories and movies about other's journeys is partly because we want to know how others handled their personal crises, health problems, and success. It means searching for the navigational tools, maps, pointers, advice, encouragement, and wisdom that helped others through life. Then we can plan our own approach to what we are facing. After all, what is most interesting is not the actual destination of the journey but everything involved in the process of getting there.

Survive and Thrive

I will be one of the first to raise my hand and admit that I want to learn how to successfully journey through life. To me, it is a lot more fun and inspiring to learn how to not only survive together, but thrive together! This is part of the reason why I decided to write this book.

If I can help others press forward in their journey, it will also bolster my own efforts to travel on the right path. The examples, stories, advice, and wisdom conveyed throughout this book offer many practical applications that anyone reading it—regardless of age, gender, ethnicity, or socioeconomic status—can use it for greater success in terms of their personal journey.

Past Journeys Help Navigate Toward Future Success

In compiling the journeys for this book, I realized more keenly that the Bible holds timeless wisdom and truths that are alive and relevant today. Although the scenery has changed since the biblical journeys took place, and the actors are different, the truths and lessons remain the same. I have also incorporated modern-day stories of amazing people who have benefited from these truths and applied them to their own personal journeys in a way that enriched their spiritual, personal, and professional development.

As you read through these journeys, take the time to see how you identify with each person by placing yourself in the shoes of those who took on the challenges and obstacles set before them. Of course, depending on where you are in your personal journey, you will most likely connect with some more than others. However, the lessons learned are vital in helping you achieve personal and spiritual breakthrough, enabling you to step onto the next path of your life travels. The beauty of these journeys is that we can all find some point of connection that will help us ponder our steps more thoughtfully, plan our direction more carefully, and bring us closer to discovering our life's adventure, destiny, and the heart of Father God.

PACK YOUR BAGS!

Someone once said, "You'll never discover new worlds unless you have courage to lose sight of the shore." If you allow the fear of the unknown to keep you from moving ahead, then you run the risk of missing some beautiful scenery, some amazing people, and some invaluable lessons. Of course, there will be challenges and obstacles as well as aggravations and mishaps; however, the experience is well worth them!

Are you packed and ready? Grab your spiritual GPS, your suitcase, and your spirit for adventure. Please join me as we take this exciting, enlightening journey together. We will build some great memories, and I think you will be pleasantly surprised by what you learn in the process.

Chapter 1

Not to Be Denied—
A Journey of Determination

The journey of a thousand miles begins with one step.
—Lao-Tzu

THERE was a story of a young journalist who was hoping to make it big, but there were not many exciting stories to cover where he lived. One day, the dam broke and the entire little town was flooded. The young man thinks this must be his big break, so he begins searching the town to nail down the story. When he spots a woman sitting on her roof, the journalist joins her there as the floodwaters rise. He explains his search. The woman responds that she is not his big story, she is just trying to survive. All of a sudden she sees a refrigerator floating by and tells him that is a story. No, that's not what he is looking for. They continue sitting, and soon an entire family clutching pieces of plywood float by. That family has to be the story—but he insists that there is something larger on the horizon. A few minutes later, an entire house floats by and she insists that it must be his story. He continues to wait. Then he sees a hat float by, but the hat stops, turns around, and goes back upstream. The hat stops and turns around again—this happens over and over. "This is my story," he tells her. "Nah, that's just my husband, Harry. He's determined to mow the grass come hell or high water."

A SENSE OF DETERMINATION

In the dictionary, *determination* is defined as a firmness of purpose or resoluteness. The *journey* of determination is a key trip that everyone needs to take during this point in history. "No time like the present" has been more important in terms of allowing determination to rise up inside of us. We must be resolute in our mission to accomplish everything that God has called us to accomplish.

Determination is the result of desperation and expectation mixed together. Desperation plus expectation produces a determination for breakthrough. There are those who have expectations that God is going to do something, but they are not really desperate for the things of the Lord. We have to have a combination of both in order to see the place of resoluteness that leads us to say, "I will take hold of those things that God has told me to take hold of."

There is a great story that came out of the 1992 Olympics held in Barcelona, Spain. A British runner, Derrick Redmond, was completely determined to finish what he had started. He was in great shape and had a strong possibility of winning a medal. However, as he ran on the track, he heard a pop. He had pulled his hamstring. At the time, he was quoted as saying, "When the pain sort of died down, I remembered where I was and what I was doing—the Olympic semifinals. Get up and start running." Derrick struggled back to his feet as the massive crowd watched, and the other runners crossed the finish line.

As Derrick hobbled along, his dad appeared on the track, having come down from the stands, and implored him to stop. It was to no avail because Derrick wanted to finish. His dad put his arm around his son, supporting him as he made his way down the track. It is an image that was replayed many times by the media, and one that stays in my mind. No one wants to see an athlete go through that type of struggle. It was obvious how devastating it was to him because of how much that race meant to him. But although he lost the race, the greater victory was his determination that pushed him across the finish line to the roar of the spectators.

Derrick's experience is a great story about determination. No matter how determined we are to cross the finish line, we need a dad to come alongside of us and support us and help us get there. Each of us has a heavenly Father that is ready at a moment's notice to come alongside of us, support us, and get us across the finish line.[1]

A DETERMINED WOMAN FROM BIBLICAL TIMES

Mark 5 tells the story of a woman who is completely determined to cross the finish line. She is extremely determined to see breakthrough in her life.

> *So Jesus went with him. A large crowd followed and pressed around Him. And a woman was there who had been subject to bleeding for twelve years. She had suffered a great deal under the care of many doctors and had spent all she had, yet instead of getting better she grew worse. When she heard about Jesus, she came up behind Him in the crowd and touched His cloak, because she thought, "If I just touch His clothes, I will be healed." Immediately her bleeding stopped and she felt in her body that she was freed from her suffering* (Mark 5:24-29).

Here is a woman who is very firm in her purpose, and she is determined that she will experience an end to her ailment and suffering. In order to understand the degree of determination that this woman has, there are a few things that you must know about her.

First of all, she is a Jewish woman. It is important to understand that, in the Jewish culture of her day, women were not really valued in society. They were not looked on as being equal to men. Jewish women were looked down upon and viewed as less than others in society. Jesus brought about a paradigm shift that so that women were valued and esteemed in the Body of Christ and in culture.

So not only is she a woman who is looked down on because of her gender, but to make matters worse, she also has had a blood disease for 12 years. The King James Version of the Bible calls it an "issue of blood," meaning she was unclean in the Jewish culture. Tradition requires that she publicly announce her unclean state when in the presence of others so that no one else is defiled. This woman is humiliated; she is full of shame; and she cannot lead a normal life. It is not possible for her to worship with others. She probably cannot have children. This woman cannot interact with others or go into the marketplace. On top of being a Jewish woman with a blood disease and suffering physically for so long, she is also financially broke. Mark 5:26 says, *"She had suffered a great deal under the care of many doctors and had spent all she had, yet instead of getting better she grew worse."*

COMPARING YOUR JOURNEY OF DETERMINATION

Have you ever been at a stage in your life where you really put your faith out there to be tested? Did you really pray and believe that something was going to change? Maybe God was going to heal your relationship. Or it could be that God was going to prosper your business. You may have prayed that God would heal your body or bring your kids back from a place of rebellion and restore them to a proper relationship. However, instead of things getting better, they got worse. Many believers have been there, and it is during these times when our faith is in jeopardy of being shipwrecked.

This is the exact place where the woman in Mark 5 found herself. There is a sense of desperation in her—there is nothing left for her to do. She has no more money. She has already been subjected to humiliation and shame. What more can she do?

Maybe that is where you find yourself. Perhaps, you have come to the end of yourself, to the end of your resources, and are now at a place where you are desperate for God. Keep in mind that desperation plus expectation produces determination for a breakthrough.

Desperation plus expectation produces determination for a breakthrough.

The Jewish woman is desperate, but she is also expecting something to change. This feeling produces determination inside of her to experience a breakthrough. Mark 5:27-28 says, *"When she heard about Jesus, she came up behind Him in the crowd and touched His cloak, because she thought, 'If I just touch His clothes, I will be healed.'"* There are several things that are interesting about this passage. First of all, she did not say, "If Jesus will touch me." Normally, if you are sick and you have heard about all of the miracles that Jesus was doing, then your first inclination would be to find a way to get to Him so that He could touch and heal you. Yet, the Jewish woman's first thought was that she wanted to touch *Him*. So many times in our lives, we think it is all about Him touching us. I think there are situations when the Lord says, "How about *you* touching *Me*?" I have discovered that, in the process of touching Him, He will touch you right back. Sometimes He waits for us to reach for Him and become desperate for Him.

Since Jesus was touching people with His hands, it would make sense that maybe she would want to grab His hand. After all, it was His hands that helped a man to see, straightened a woman who was hunched over, and raised a little boy from the dead. So why does she want to touch His clothes? In her day, Jewish men wore an undergarment that was like a long t-shirt known as a tunic. This was worn around the house and out in the fields, but it was not allowed in the synagogue—there they wore another garment that went over their shoulders and was fastened with a belt. Known as a *tallit*, it was rectangular shaped and had tassels that hung from the four corners. These garments were very significant for Jewish men, as seen in Numbers 15:37-39:

> *The Lord said to Moses, "Speak to the Israelites and say to them: Throughout the generations to come you are to make tassels on the corners of your garments, with a blue cord on each tassel. You will have these tassels to look at and so you will remember all the commands of the Lord...."*

In each tassel, there were five knots. These five knots were symbolic of the first five books of the Bible, or what the Jews call the Torah. When they wore their tallit, they saw these tassels every single day. They reminded them of the law of the Lord and the Scriptures.

What is interesting to note is that there is a Hebrew word, *kanaf,* which means corner, or tassel. The plural is *kanafot,* which also means wing. This word is used in Malachi 4:2:

> *But for you who revere my name, the sun of righteousness will rise with healing in its wings. And you will go out and leap like calves released from the stall* (Malachi 4:2).

While you may think of wings that overshadow you and wings of healing, the Jewish people thought about the tassels. To them, and according to the Old Testament prophet Malachi, the Messiah would come; and when He did, there would be healing in His wings, or tassels.

So, why does this Jewish woman want to touch His clothes and not His hands? She firmly believes that Jesus has healing in the tassels of His tallit. That is why she is determined that, in some way, she will press through and touch the tassels. Although it may seem like there is nothing special about touching this clothing other than its meaning, her understanding is that this is how she will receive healing. While we believe that the healing is in the Messiah, this woman is sure that the healing was in the tassels.

Out of desperation and expectation, she is determined to find a way to touch His tassels. Remember that desperation plus expectation produces a determination for breakthrough. She needs a breakthrough. She is desperate. She is expecting. She is determined that she is going to get to Him.

There are two key words in the story that need special attention. The first word is *crowd*. It is not like there are only 10 or 15 people gathered around Jesus. There is a throng of people who are pressing against Him. There is a good chance that she has had this great plan in her mind that, when the Messiah comes through, she is just going to run up, grab the tassel, and healing is going to happen. Well, sometimes the best laid plans of men—and women—fall by the wayside. When the Messiah comes through, a massive crowd of people gathers around Him. They represent a great obstacle and barrier for the woman. Often, when we have a plan from God and things do not go the way we envision, we are quick to just give up and say, "I didn't hear from God; it's not worth it; or, things will never change."

Here is a woman who is looking at a massive crowd around Jesus and she is faced with a decision. She most likely ponders, *What do I do? Is it worth it? Do I continue on my determined journey or maybe some other time He will come back through town and then I can touch Him?* We have to make up our minds because determination will cost us. The times we need to be the most determined is often when we feel like being less determined. When we need to be the most determined and press through obstacles and barriers, we may feel as if we can not or do not want to press on. This feeling is a good indication that breakthrough is about to come. This is when you need to dig deep and allow determination to rise up inside of you and proclaim, "Nothing will keep me from touching Him because I'm determined. I'm going to have breakthrough. And breakthrough is not just dependent on me—it involves the Lord helping me breakthrough and touching Him."

Sometimes God removes the barriers and the obstacles. When we pray for a financial breakthrough, God removes the barriers. The same

"I'm giving you the grace to press through."

can be said if there is a barrier in your marriage or business. We pray, we act, and then God removes the barriers. Don't you just love those times in your life when God removes the barriers? There are also situations when God does not remove the barriers but instead provides you with the grace, strength, and mercy to face them.

You may be at this point right now in your life where you have been waiting on God to remove the barrier so you can make progress. However, God tells you, "I'm giving you the grace to press through." For this Jewish woman, the crowd is the barrier for her, and she has to make the decision to press on because the crowd is not leaving. She has to decide if it is worth fighting her way through the crowd.

The second thing that we notice is the word *touch*. Touch is a key concept because here is a woman who thinks, "I have nothing to lose and everything to gain. I might as well go for it and touch Him. I'm going to touch Him and, in the process of touching Him, I am going to believe that He is going to touch me." It is easy to form a mental picture of a woman who is determined that she is going to receive relief. She is determined that she is going to fight her way through the crowd but, in order to do that, she has to be willing to let go of her doubts.

Have you heard the voice of doubt? Those nagging voices constantly telling you that you will never be healed. Your marriage will never change. Your finances will never change. You will never find true joy. You will never overcome the addiction. Your kids will never come back to the Lord. You will never experience a spiritual breakthrough. Those voices of doubt constantly whisper in your ear. Therefore, it is easy to imagine at that moment the Jewish woman is looking at this massive crowd and she hears the voices of doubt in her head saying that she will never get to Him.

However, she pushes aside the voices of doubt—just like you have to do—and fights her way through the crowd. Imagine seeing her on hands and knees with dust coming up in her face and people bumping and kicking her. She has every reason to turn back. Yet, she is fighting her way through the crowd to reach those tassels until she is just inches away. At that point, the Jewish woman reaches out and touches the tassels. The Bible says that she is immediately healed—not because of the cloth, but because of the Man the cloth was draped over. Immediately, her body is healed, and she is made completely new. Why? Because she vowed not to give up or veer from her journey of determination.

CADEN'S STORY

It was November 7, 2006, and we were desperate for a breakthrough. Our youngest son was born September 20, 2006, weighing just 1 lb., 11oz and measuring a little over 12 inches in length. He was rushed to the NICU at Presbyterian Hospital in Charlotte to begin a difficult tug-of-war between life and death. Surrounded by skilled doctors and nurses, and millions of dollars of medical equipment, we were determined to see life win the battle.

The journey started out well, but complications set in around week 4. Medical terms we had barely heard before became a part of our daily vocabulary, and on that Tuesday, November 7th, the doctors and nurses informed us that there was nothing left for them to attempt to see life win out. Caden was on 100 percent oxygen, his digestion was not working, and we found ourselves surrounded not only by the constant beeping of monitors and machines, but by the loud voice of hopelessness.

My wife, Melanie, reminds me of a modern-day example of the woman in Mark 5. Every single day she would make the 30-minute drive to the hospital to sit by Caden's isolette, praying over him and fighting for his life, pressing her way through doubt and discouragement, determined to touch Jesus. On this particular dismal Tuesday night, we sat together by his bed in the NICU, praying for breakthrough. As we were praying, I heard the Lord speak the word "jubilee" to my spirit.

I knew that a part of the meaning of the word and concept was that during the year of jubilee for the Israelites, things would be returned to their original owners, and land would be given a season of rest. I also commented to Melanie that Caden's fiftieth day on earth was approaching soon. We agreed together that we would begin declaring jubilee over him, that everything in his body would be returned to its original state and function, and that his body would have rest.

The next day his condition worsened. Melanie sat by his side, desperate for breakthrough. I sat at my desk at The Refuge, praying and declaring jubilee. I counted the days on my computer's calendar and discovered that November 8, that very day, was his fiftieth day on earth. We stood in faith, fighting our way through despair and hopelessness. Our daughter and other two sons were battling with us in prayer. Clay, who was seven at the time, announced to me that night that he was going to fast his next three meals for Caden's healing!

Later that evening, as we again sat by his little isolette, the nurses noticed a slight, minute change in some of his levels. And from that moment on, Caden experienced a supernatural breakthrough in his body! Everything began to function over the days following, and on his hundredth day in the NICU, we experienced a second jubilee when we took Caden home!

He is now the most vibrant, strong, athletic three-year-old I've ever seen, showing no signs of being born premature, even when examined by doctors. He is a testimony to the faithfulness of God, and to a woman who refused to quit, who sat every single day for 100 days at his bedside, crawled past the obstacles, and touched Jesus.

ARE YOU DESPERATE AND EXPECTANT FOR BREAKTHROUGH?

Desperation plus expectation produces determination for a breakthrough. Is there an area of your life where you need to experience breakthrough? In thinking back to the story of the Jewish woman and the inspiring miracle of Caden, look for ways to make your journey of determination as strong and faithful as those women. Even if you feel challenged and fatigued, keep moving forward! If you reach out, press through obstacles, and overcome discouragement because you are determined to touch Him, I believe that the Lord will touch you right back.

ENDNOTE

1. John E. Anderson, "What Makes Olympic Champions?" *Reader's Digest* (February 1994), p. 120.

Chapter 2

Heavenly Download—
A Journey of Impartation

No journey carries one far unless, as it extends into the world around us, it goes an equal distance into the world within.
—Lillian Smith

YOU might ask, what is impartation, and do I really want to take such a journey? It may sound kind of strange to you. When I think of impartation, there are many different images that come to mind. The main one that pops up is of some guy trying to navigate a steep climb up a mountain to reach a temple. He is trying to get to a guru who has the ability to impart knowledge to him.

The word *impart* means to bestow or to give a share of something. This situation happens to each and every one of us on a daily basis. We are constantly imparted with various things by the people who surround us. Whether it is a colleague at work, the media, a teacher at school, or our friends, we are bombarded with information. For example, a financial advisor can impart wisdom about IRAs or mutual funds. You might have someone impart knowledge about creating a healthier lifestyle, while someone else might impart kindness into your life.

A Spiritual Impartation

There is also a higher power—the Lord, Himself—who wants to impart His spirit and His anointing into your life. There really is no greater impartation than that. Do you feel that you need more of the Lord in your life? The good news—God wants to, and will, impart Himself into you. When you think about it, it is one thing for someone to impart knowledge or kindness, but it is an entirely different matter for the God of the universe to impart His heart or His anointing into you. That is a truly amazing thing! Genesis 32:22-30 is where the story of impartation begins with Jacob:

> *That night Jacob got up and took his two wives, his two maidservants and his eleven sons and crossed the ford of the Jabbok. After he had sent them across the stream, he sent over all his possessions. So Jacob was left alone, and a man wrestled with him till daybreak. When the man saw that He could not overpower him, He touched the socket of Jacob's hip so that his hip was wrenched as he wrestled with the man. Then the man said, "Let Me go, for it is daybreak." But Jacob replied, "I will not let You go unless You bless me." The man asked him, "What is your name?" "Jacob," he answered. Then the man said, "Your name will no longer be Jacob, but Israel, because you have struggled with God and with men and have overcome." Jacob said, "Please tell me Your name." But he replied, "Why do you ask My name?" Then He blessed him there. So Jacob called the place Peniel, saying, "It is because I saw God face to face, and yet my life was spared" (Genesis 32:22-30).*

In order to truly understand what was involved in Jacob's journey of impartation, it is important to go back a few chapters to Genesis 25. Here, we read the story of twins, Jacob and Esau. Jacob tricks his brother and convinces him to sell his birthright, which was given to Esau because he was born first. Esau agrees to do this simply for a bowl of stew. Jacob also deceives his father, Isaac, into blessing him instead of Esau. Jacob does this by taking animal skins and placing them over his arms to give the impression that he is hairy like Esau. Because Jacob's father is old, his eyesight has failed him. He says that the voice sounds like that of Jacob but that the arms feel like that of Esau. Isaac blesses Jacob and Esau becomes so furious that he plots to kill Jacob after their father dies. Rebecca, his mother, overhears the plot and convinces Jacob to go live with his uncle, Laban, as detailed in Genesis 28.

For the next 15 years, the twins do not see or have any communication with each other. In Genesis 31, Jacob has a dream in which the Lord speaks to him and tells him that he must return to his homeland and make things right with Esau. Despite the imminent threat of death, Genesis 32 says that Jacob obeys God. He gathers all the wealth that he has accumulated, leaves Laban, and goes back to try and make things right with Esau. Jacob sends word to let him know that he is coming home. The Bible says that Esau comes out to meet him with 400 men. This makes Jacob very fearful, so he sends wave after wave of gifts to Esau to soften him up. The Bible says that Jacob remains in the camp, awaiting a response. What Jacob does not realize is that God has arranged for a divine impartation that he does not even know he needs.

There are times in our lives when God sets us up in an unexpected way. Have you ever experienced a situation where you are not looking for anything and do not even know that you need anything, but God divinely interrupts your life and imparts something into you that forever changes you? That happens not only with salvation, but it also occurs after salvation in different seasons and times in our lives. This is because God has a storehouse of things

> Sometimes God arranges for a divine impartation that you don't even know you need.

that He desires to impart into our lives even if we do not know that we need them.

A MODERN-DAY JOURNEY OF IMPARTATION

James Dobson is best known for his Focus on the Family ministry, headquartered at an expansive campus in Colorado Springs, Colorado. Started in a small office in Arcadia, California, in 1977, Dobson's ministry has spread worldwide and is managed by a team of thousands. While many may be familiar with his ministry, very few may know the story of James Dobson's father, James Dobson Sr.

Before James Dobson's dad was even five years old, he told everyone that he was going to grow up to be a great artist. He loved to draw and had an amazing talent. He envisioned himself as the next Rembrandt or Michelangelo. His plans for the future were set. When he was 16 years of age, he was walking down the street and felt a voice come from deep down inside him, "I want you to prepare your life for full-time ministry." Because he thought that he knew what God already wanted him to do, he chose to ignore the voice. Yet, over the next several months and years, the voice returned.

On the last day of high school, he heard the voice again, "Today, you will have to decide." So all throughout the day, he wrestled with this decision. His dad had already told him that he would send him to any college that he wanted. At the end of the day, he returned to an empty house. Dobson's dad pointed his finger to the ceiling and, in an act of defiance, said, "I will not do it because it will cost too much."

Dobson's dad said that the moment after was one of the most horrible moments of his life. He said that he literally felt the spirit of God leave him. Soon after that, his mother came home and she found her son pale and anguished, so she asked him what was wrong. He told her that he had forsaken God and related how he had wrestled over his decision. She felt that he was overreacting and suggested that they pray. All of a sudden, in the midst of praying, James Dobson's grandmother stopped and said, "Something is wrong." He told her that he had tried to tell her that he knew that the spirit of God had left him.

It would be seven years before he would hear the voice of God again. Meanwhile, he enrolled in the Art Institute of Pittsburgh, one of the most prestigious art schools in the nation. All of the professors immediately recognized his incredible gift for art, and he was voted as the most talented artist at the school. After he graduated, the Great Depression arrived. The only job he found as a college graduate was washing windshields and pumping gas.

Every now and then, he would recall the voice he had heard as a teenager and would mull over the decision that he had made. In the meantime, the president of the Art Institute wrote a letter, inviting him to come and join the faculty for $300 a month, which, at that time, was an enormous amount of money. Somehow, the letter got lost on the president's desk and was never mailed. At the same time, Dobson's dad decided to finally surrender his life to the agenda and plan of life that God had already told him about. Around the same time, the president of the Art Institute also found the letter and mailed it to him, but it was too late. Dobson's dad responded that he had other plans.

James Dobson's dad pursued full-time ministry and, because of that, James Dobson's life was shaped for founding a worldwide ministry that has immeasurable impact. What was imparted to Dobson's father could not be imparted until there was a moment of surrender. What was imparted to Dobson's dad went from him to his son James. For Dads who are reading this book, you have a great responsibility resting on your shoulders. It involves surrendering to the Lord in such a way that God can impart things into your lives. If you allow this to happen, then you can impart these into your sons and daughters, but it must come through surrender.[1]

OPEN UP YOURSELF TO IMPARTATION

The Bible gives three things that you have to do or possess in order for impartation from God to take place in your life: surrender; unity; struggle.

1. There is an element of surrender.

Genesis 32:22 says, *"That night Jacob got up and took his two wives, his two maidservants and his eleven sons and crossed the ford of the Jabbok."* The word Jabbok means to pour out, make empty, or void. In order for there to be an impartation from the Lord, something has to leave or go out of us so that there is room for God to impart something into our lives. This is the element of surrender. It involves emptying ourselves of self and pouring out anything that would inhibit the flow of God's anointing or impartation. Addison Leitch said, "When the will of God crosses the will of man, somebody has to die."[2]

In order for there to be impartation in your life, something in you has to die. God's plan for you is not to necessarily remove things from you; it actually involves putting more of Himself in you. John understood the concept of impartation when he said in John 3:30: *"He must become greater; I must become less."* That element of surrender creates space and makes room for the Lord. When we surrender our agendas, plans, dreams, lives, egos, minds, futures, failures, and shortcomings to the Lord, we gain the opportunity of having God bestow something—a part of Himself—on our lives.

2. There is unity with your brothers and sisters.

It is absolutely essential that you are in unity with your brothers and sisters in order for God to impart His nature, His heart, and His anointing into your life. God spoke to Jacob in a dream and told him to go back to his homeland so that he could make things right with Esau, his brother. It was only when Jacob obeyed God that He arranged for the impartation. As you obey God in the area of unity, reconciling with those who you are at odds with or bringing unity to those with whom you have had a falling out, He will then arrange for the impartation of His anointing and the impartation of His heart into your heart.

Unity is an essential tool in your life because God cannot bring His heart into a life of disunity. If you are not in unity with others and the anointing of God's Spirit is blocked in your life, it stops the flow of God's anointing throughout the community and the city. God is not just about one little castle. He is about expressing His kingdom throughout the

> When you surrender your agendas, plans, dreams, lives, egos, minds, futures, failures, and shortcomings to the Lord, you gain the opportunity of having God bestow part of Himself in your life.

entire city, community, and world. The responsibility then rests on you and me, as individuals, to make sure that we are not blocking this anointing so that others can also be set free through His impartation.

Unity is not just something that we can muster up or that we create on our own. It is the work of the Holy Spirit. Acts 2 is a great example of the impartation of the anointing of God that comes through unity. The disciples and others had been instructed to go to an upper room in Jerusalem and wait for an impartation of the Lord. The Bible says that, when they were in unity, the impartation of the Holy Spirit came. It took all of them joining together to make that happen.

To give you a great visual example, imagine a room full of pianos. One hundred pianos need to be tuned. You decide to take one piano that was in tune and you tuned the other to that one and so on until you went through every piano in the room. Guess what? Every one of them would be out of tune. However, if you tuned all one hundred pianos to one tuning fork, then all of the pianos would be in tune. The lesson here is that we cannot create unity just in ourselves by saying, "Let's join hands and sing some ballad that brings tears to our eyes and then we'll be in unity." On the contrary, we have to tune our lives, individually, to Christ, which puts us in harmony and unity with each other. An excellent Scripture reinforcing this idea is in Psalm 133:

> *How good and pleasant it is when brothers live together in unity! It is like precious oil poured on the head, running down on the beard, running down on Aaron's beard, down upon the collar of his robes. It is as if the dew of Hermon were falling on Mount Zion. For there the Lord bestows His blessing, even life forevermore* (Psalm 133:1-3).

It is when we desire unity with the Lord that God brings unity to each of us and that is the point at which the Lord imparts His anointing. When we are in harmony with each other and with others in the Body of Christ—even though they may be of a different denomination and there may be some differences in the way we approach the journey with the Lord—there can still be a release of the anointing of God across a city and a community. This is because God desires to transform whole cities and entire communities through the impartation of His anointing. That will not come unless we surrender our lives and decide to tune our lives to that of the Lord.

Each Wednesday morning, I meet with a group of pastors from different churches in our city to pray for unity and the move of God. The name of our city, Concord, literally means "harmony." We are striving through prayer for the unity that Jesus prays for in John 17, a unity that will bring an outpouring of the Spirit of God. Recently, a well-known prophet in the land by the name of Bob Jones sat with this group of pastors, along with other leaders in the city, to share the things God has been stirring in his heart concerning our city. I believe these prophetic stirrings and the increase of the release of God's anointing in our city are the result of this unified prayer offered each week.

3. A struggle is required for transformation.

Nothing in life that is really worth having is easy. That is why it is so important and poignant that Jacob experienced a wrestling match with God. There is a struggle when we have an impartation from the Lord. If we do not understand that there is a struggle, then we will be disappointed and disillusioned because we will completely miss the impartation.

We cannot question God by saying, "Hey, God, I thought You were going to impart this identity to me. I thought I was going to do something great for You. You spoke this Word over my life and now it has not occurred." This attitude occurs frequently regarding healing. For example, God says that He is going to heal someone; the Word comes and there is healing and power—but the healing does not manifest immediately. That is because there must be a struggle for the impartation that has not yet occurred with the person who is waiting to receive it.

> Be careful what you speak over your children because it may be the very impartation of their destiny—whether you intend it or not.

The story about helping a butterfly escape its cocoon too quickly without the prerequisite struggle, illustrates the point perfectly. The butterfly's struggle builds up the muscle strength necessary for it to live and take flight.

A struggle will occur during transformation on the journey of impartation. It is a struggle to find flight. When we are aware that these events are part of what we must go through, then we can expect them, look into the circumstances of our lives, and see God at work when difficulty occurs. We can visualize a curse turning into a blessing. In Romans 8:28, Paul says, *"And we know that in all things God works for the good of those who love Him, who have been called according to His purpose."* This applies to all things and every circumstance. Life's difficulties are simply part of the struggle to bring impartation to our lives.

APPLICATION FROM JACOB'S JOURNEY

Three things in the life of Jacob illustrate just how much of a struggle it can be for us in our own lives in order to receive this impartation: limp; lie; and lifestyle.

1. He received a limp.

Jacob wrestled with God, and, during the struggle, God touched his hip and Jacob developed a limp. The hip symbolizes an area of self-reliance. God wants us to deal with any struggle by relying on ourselves in order to make ourselves ready to lean on Him for this impartation. Look at your body. It is your hip that supports your weight. Without one, you cannot stand on your own. Jacob, from that point on, walked with a limp to show that he could not do it on his own. He was imparted something and God became his reliance. He could not stand on his own because he had wrestled with God. Jacob's limp represented the end of self-reliance.

2. He addressed the lie.

Genesis 32:27 says, *"The man asked him, 'What is your name?' 'Jacob,' he answered."* This interchange is interesting because it is similar to what happened years before when Jacob asked his father for the blessing. God wanted to address Jacob's past and the lie that he told. The name *Jacob* means trickster. Jacob was raised hearing that he was a trickster, a liar, and a schemer. In reality, Jacob fulfilled the destiny found within his name. Parent, be careful what you speak over your children because it may be the very impartation of their destiny whether you intend it or not. When Jacob met with God for this impartation of his identity, the angel of the Lord asked him who he was and he responded that he was Jacob. The angel of God responded that Jacob was to have a new name and—he would be called Israel. Because of Jacob's honesty, he was told he would be blessed and become the nation that he had heard his grandfather, Abraham, talk about. Jacob was told that he was going to be the father of the 12 tribes.

It is interesting to note that this encounter changed Jacob's destiny and his identity. Genesis 35:18 says that Jacob's wife, Rachel, was about to give birth to their son but she was having trouble. As Rachel was taking her last breath because she was dying, she named her son Ben-Oni, which means son of my trouble. However, Jacob stepped in because he remembered what it was like to be called a trickster. He did not want his son to be named Ben-Oni and to suffer the meaning. Instead, he spoke a blessing over his son and named him Benjamin, which means son of my right hand. Jacob does the same thing for his son as God did for him in terms of blessing him and changing his name.

I believe that God was saying that if we fail to identify the lie in our life, then that lie will identify us. When God gives us the impartation of this destiny and this identity, we have got to identify the struggle and the lie. We must get over our self-reliance with the limp and acknowledge any lies we are telling ourselves or others.

3. He entered a new lifestyle.

From that moment on, Jacob walked with a limp. When his family saw him coming, they knew that there was something different. After his wrestle with God, he had to live out his new identity on a daily basis. He was no longer Jacob. He was Israel, with a limp.

If you are a young person, you need to know that you have a destiny—a greatness—that has been spoken over your generation. This greatness is faithfulness, consistency, and character. That is the impartation. By now the circumstances you have experienced have developed your character and struggles have built you up so that your eyes are focused on Him and you are not lost in your own greatness. You are so focused on the Lord that you may not even see that He has done something amazing in your life. Never deny that there will be a struggle. Expect it. Anticipate it. And count on God to bring you victoriously through each struggle.

Straighten Out and Own Up

When there is impartation from the Lord in your life, it will bring about permanent changes just like it did for Jacob, resulting in a limp and different name. Sometimes the change happens on the inside. However, before that can happen, you must realize that God will not bless your messed-up life. Jacob had to straighten out his life. It was only when Jacob owned up to who he was that he could become who God wanted him to be. If you are willing to own up to who you really are, then God can release you into who He wants you to be by imparting His heart and His anointing.

Your status in the world will not get you a heavenly download. Jacob was a prosperous guy and had amassed great wealth. You can be very successful in life. You can be a great businessperson. You can climb the corporate ladder. You can have a wonderful family. You can have an amazing career. But at the same time you can be bankrupt spiritually and have no anointing whatsoever in your life. Externally and internally, God wants to bless your spirit and your heart. He wants to increase His nature, His heart, and His anointing in your life. However, it will only come when you are willing to surrender, when you are willing to be unified with your brothers and sisters, and when you are willing to fight for your destiny.

There is no quick fix. One church service each week does not guarantee you will receive impartation from God and have your life transformed. Most likely, it will cost you much more than that—wrestling and numerous struggles. Receiving impartation involves coming to grips with who you really are, owning up to it, and acknowledging that God is right. For example, you might have to say, "Yes, I am an adulterer. I am dishonest. I am a thief. I do lack integrity." By admitting any and all of these characteristics that define who you are now, God can then transform you into the man or woman of God that He has always known and wanted.

THE BEAUTY OF IMPARTATION

After the impartation occurs in your life, there is a beauty that exudes from your dramatic transformation. In returning to Jacob's journey of impartation, let's consider Esau who wanted to kill Jacob, his brother. However, the Bible says that when Esau saw Israel coming—the new Jacob—he saw such a visible change that he did not want to kill him.

What did he want to do? Esau wanted to embrace him. (See Genesis 33:4.)

For so long, the church has walked in arrogance and pride which has repelled the world. It is not enough to just be touched by God. We need to be changed. When God imparts His heart and His anointing and we reach the place where we can be authentic in the Lord, we can admit to who we are and become transformed from the inside out. Only then will others notice a visible change. The effect can transform others who had previously been skeptical so that they become filled with the desire to embrace us and the community of believers.

If we are transformed, the world will really be embracing Christ. Impartation makes a visible change that comes from the anointing of the Lord. We have to empty ourselves and surrender to God. That involves pouring out the good, the bad, *and* the ugly. Then, you must remove any disunity that you have with others in your life by making things right with them. From there, you have to be willing to fight, to struggle, and to wrestle for the destiny that is inherent in the impartation of God.

ENDNOTES

1. James C. Dobson and J. Vernon McGee, *Life on the Edge* (Nashville, TN: Thomas Nelson Publishers, 2000). http://net.bible.org/illustration.php?topic=365.

2. Ibid.

Chapter 3

I Didn't See This Coming!—A Journey of Obedience

Life begins as a quest of the child for the man and ends as a journey by the man to rediscover the child.
—Laurens van der Post

IN the 1970s, Roger Staubach was an NFL quarterback for the Dallas Cowboys. He was an intelligent guy coached by a brilliant man named Tom Landry. What upset Roger Staubach was the fact that Coach Landry would not let him call his own plays. Every single play was sent into the huddle by Coach Landry. This challenged the great quarterback's ego like a medieval jouster who was charging head on toward him. It became an issue of pride for Staubach. However, he made a statement that is important to the idea of obedience when he said, "I faced up to the issue of obedience. Once I learned to obey, there was harmony, fulfillment, and victory."[1] When you face the issue of obedience in your life, then you will be rewarded with harmony, fulfillment, and victory. Thomas Kempis said, "Whoever strives to withdraw from obedience—withdraws from grace."[2]

One important Bible story where obedience led to harmony, fulfillment, and victory was that of Jonah. This was one of my favorite stories that my grandmother would tell me at bedtime as a young boy. At that point in my life, I thought Jonah's story was just a cool, adventure tale about a guy who ends up in the belly of a whale. Now, I realize that Jonah is an incredible real-life example of the journey of obedience.

PART ONE OF JONAH'S JOURNEY: ORDER, OBJECTION, AND ORDEAL

Jonah's journey was not easy:

> *The word of the Lord came to Jonah son of Amittai: "Go to the great city of Nineveh and preach against it, because its wickedness has come up before me." But Jonah ran away from the Lord and headed for Tarshish. He went down to Joppa, where he found a ship bound for that port. After paying the fare, he went aboard and sailed for Tarshish to flee from the Lord* (Jonah 1:1-3).

The first part of Jonah's journey is summed up with: order; objection; and ordeal.

1. The order came.

The order came from the Lord that Jonah was to go to Nineveh and preach against the wickedness that was occurring there. The order was quite clear, and Jonah knew what to do.

2. He raised an objection.

Knowing what to do and wanting to do it were two entirely different things for Jonah. Although he received crystal-clear instructions from the Lord, Jonah did not agree with the order. Jonah did not like the city of Nineveh because he was aware of the Assyrian's reputation for being a cruel and wicked people who posed a great threat to the nation of Israel. He knew they had erected monuments to themselves, detailing the way they tortured and murdered anyone who opposed them. It is easy to understand Jonah's hesitation because of the likelihood of being killed. He did the exact opposite of what the Lord ordered him to do by purchasing a ticket that took him as far away from his God-given task in Nineveh as possible.

3. He faced the ordeal.

It was Jonah's decision to object that set him on the path to his ordeal. Jonah 1:4 states: *"Then the Lord sent a great wind on the sea, and such a violent storm arose that the ship threatened to break up."* The sailors— often thought of as some of the bravest men—were gripped with fear, according to Jonah 1:5 because they were sure that the violent storm was going to pull their ship apart.

Your Journey of Obedience

Before following Jonah any further on his journey of obedience, think about your own life. Has there been a time in your life when God told you clearly to do something or to not do something? It could be that God said: "Do not date that person. Do not buy that house. Do not take that job." You may have heard a clear word from God, but you did not like what He said and you ignored His word.

Like Jonah, you may have formed an objection by doing the exact opposite of what you were told by the Lord. He told you not to take the job, and what do you do? You might have accepted the job. He said not to marry that person, and what did you do? You might have married that person, and now you are divorced. God said not to date that person, and what did you do? You dated that person and ended up being hurt. God told you not to buy that vehicle, and you purchased it anyway. Because of our carnal nature, human beings are prone to doing the opposite of what we know God wants us to do.

LIVING IN DISOBEDIENCE PRODUCES APATHY

While you consider your own journey of obedience, think about what happened to Jonah when he diverged from the path and became disobedient. The sailors knew that someone on the ship was responsible for their ordeal with the storm, so they began casting lots to find the answer. During this time, Jonah had gone below deck and fallen asleep. Despite the storm, the chaos, and the activity, Jonah was not affected. How could he sleep when there was a storm that threatened to take his life?

When people decide to exist within a disobedient life, they arrive at a destination of apathy. Hence, disobedience produces apathy. When we are living in disobedience, we are usually the first ones to know it. Nobody has to tell us that we are disobeying God. We do not need someone else to tell us that we are rebelling. When we are disobedient, it is clear that we are objecting to what God has told us to do by heading in the opposite direction. Often, we do not want to be confronted with the truth. We may say, "I know that I'm living in rebellion. I know that I'm disobeying God, but I don't want to come face to face with that." Jonah knew he was living in rebellion—that he was disobedient to God—so he pretended like the ordeal did not exist. He tried to shut himself in and not confront the peril by opting to sleep.

This life of disobedience and apathy describes our society today. A situation captured on a surveillance camera in Hartford, Connecticut, provides an excellent example of how many people have become desensitized and apathetic. A 78-year-old man stepped off the curb and walked into the street, but he failed to see an oncoming car. The car struck him, threw his body up into the air, and he landed in the middle of the street, bleeding profusely from his head. The car that hit him never stopped.

Another ten cars passed his body and even swerved around his body, but none of them stopped!

The surveillance camera showed a sidewalk full of people, but it took quite a few minutes before anyone checked on his condition. When people were interviewed and asked why they would let a 78-year-old man lie in the middle of the road bleeding to death, they responded that it was a crime-ridden area and they had become accustomed to a culture that does not care.[3]

That attitude describes today's society. Do not make eye contact. Do not ask the right questions or the wrong questions. Do not get involved in the situation. In fact, we will disobey God so not to become involved in someone else's life. However, Dr. P.J. Miller said, "It is a great deal easier to do what God gives us to do—no matter how hard it is—than face the responsibility of not doing it."[4]

Likewise, Jonah was apathetic to the whole stormy sea situation. He did not want to take responsibility for his disobedience. In the back of his mind, Jonah knew the consequences of disobeying God far outweighed the difficulty of what he had been called to do in Nineveh. When the sailors confronted Jonah, he admitted that he was running from God and that he was responsible for the storm. Jonah told them to throw him overboard and the storm would stop. The sailors did not want to take his life but the storm got worse, so they prayed to God that they would not be responsible for Jonah's death and tossed him into the sea. As soon as they did, the sea became calm and the storm ceased. (See Jonah 1:12-15.)

PART TWO OF JONAH'S JOURNEY:
DESPAIR, DEDICATION, AND DELIVERANCE

Those of you reading this book may have found yourself in a similar place as Jonah—the pit of despair. The second half of his journey focused on three aspects: despair, dedication, and deliverance.

Jonah was trapped in the belly of a fish with bile, seaweed, and half-digested fish. He had hit rock bottom and was in a very bad state:

> From inside the fish Jonah prayed to the Lord his God. He said: "In my distress I called to the Lord, and He answered me. From the depths of the grave I called for help, and You listened to my cry" (Jonah 2:1-2).

The prayer continues in Jonah 2:3-10:

> You hurled me into the deep, into the very heart of the seas, and the currents swirled about me; all Your waves and breakers swept over me. I said, "I have been banished from Your sight; yet I will look again toward Your holy temple. The engulfing waters threatened me, the deep surrounded me; seaweed was wrapped around my head. To the roots of the mountains I sank down; the earth beneath barred me in forever. But You brought my life up from the pit, O Lord my God. When my life was ebbing away, I remembered You, Lord, and my prayer rose to You, to your holy temple. Those who cling to worthless idols forfeit the grace that could be theirs. But I, with a song of thanksgiving, will sacrifice to You. What I have vowed I will make good. Salvation comes from the Lord." And the Lord commanded the fish, and it vomited Jonah onto dry land.

This passage illustrates Jonah's change of heart and his dedication to return to the journey of obedience, which led to his deliverance in verse 10.

YOUR PATH TO DELIVERANCE

It should make you happy to know that, when you are in trouble or distress, the Lord will answer your prayer. Ask yourself if you are excited about the prospects surrounding your own salvation. The answer should be a resounding yes, especially since it is clear in Jonah 3 how many chances God gives us. Ask yourself if you are thankful for the numerous chances that God has given you in your life.

> When you are in trouble or distress, the Lord will answer your prayer.

Jonah 3:1-2 illustrates how God gave Jonah another chance to obey: *"Then the word of the Lord came to Jonah a second time: 'Go to the great city of Nineveh and proclaim to it the message I give you.'"* These are some of the most comforting Scriptures in the entire Word of God. Despite our rebellious spirit or disobedience, God is faithful and comes back to us again and again when we ask for His forgiveness. When we sink into the depths of the sea, God brings His word to us again. When we are at that place in life when we hit rock bottom, we remember a Scripture that our grandmother taught us; we recollect a lesson that our Sunday school teacher taught us; or we reflect on a prayer that a friend prayed over us. The Word of the Lord comes back to us again and again.

This time, Jonah obeyed and returned to Nineveh with unexpected results. Jonah 3:5 says, *"The Ninevites believed God. They declared a fast, and all of them, from the greatest to the least, put on sackcloth."* As Jonah preached to this wicked city of over 120,000 people, a citywide transformation occurred when people started repenting and crying out to God. They declared a fast and Jonah was shocked by the response. This illustrates the importance of never underestimating the power of the Word of God.

It just goes to show that we do not get to determine the outcome. Our job is simply to obey. God has called us to be obedient and declare what He has called us to declare. His Word is powerful enough to bring the transformation, even if we think that those receiving the declaration may not be interested. After God saw that the Ninevites turned from their evil ways, He showed them compassion and did not bring the destruction that He had threatened. Jonah 3:10 says, *"When God saw what they did and how they turned from their evil ways, He had compassion and did not bring upon them the destruction He had threatened."*

Jonah's journey of obedience was a great success. A city of 120,000 people was not only spared from the wrath of God, but everyone within that city was also transformed by the power of God. It would seem as though Jonah would be excited about that. Instead, he was angry. Jonah had it all played out in his mind. He was going to obey God and go to Nineveh. He was going to preach against their wickedness, and they were going to get angry. They were not going to repent, and God was going to wipe out the whole city.

On his journey of obedience, something was exposed in Jonah's heart. Often, the things we discover on the way to the destination outweigh what we find when we arrive at the destination. As Jonah was traveling toward obedience, he was forced to come face to face with the fact that he had prejudice and hatred in his heart for the Ninevites. And although he was a messenger and conduit for the compassion of God, he had no compassion in his heart. Many times the reason the Lord selects us for an assignment is not because we are the most qualified but because we are the neediest. God recognizes something in our hearts and, in His mercy and His desire to make us more like Himself, He wants to take us on a journey of obedience.

Meanwhile, we think it is all about the other people, just as Jonah believed it was all about the Ninevites. But God said that it was about Jonah as well. So while he thought God's decision concerned only the Ninevites, he stopped and realized that he had hatred in his heart for them. This journey of obedience is about all the things that God teaches us along the way to the final destination.

In the summer of 2000, we left North Carolina after a lengthy and successful season of ministry and moved to LA (Lower Alabama). We had accepted our first senior pastor opportunity at a church outside of

Mobile. We were full of vision, energy, excitement, and ideas that we knew were certain to grow a strong church into an even stronger one. We were only the third pastor of this church in 47 years, and our vision soon began to be challenged with questions from the people like, "Why would you want to do that?" We stayed on course, loving the people God had entrusted to us, and learning many valuable but hard lessons along the way. Our nearly four years there educated us in leadership principles that helped form the foundation when we planted The Refuge.

Staying the Course

To benefit from the things God wants to teach you, how do you stay on course? Jonah veered from the course, and it was costly. It is vital to understand that your obedience or disobedience will always affect the destiny of others. The choices you make when you hear from God force you to make a decision immediately. Will I obey or will I disobey? How will my decision affect how I stay on course?

Technology has created a wonderful device called a global positioning system, or GPS. These things are amazing. You can take it anywhere in the world and it will show the streets around you, or in another city. If you want to find a restaurant, you just type in the name and the GPS directs you right to the restaurant. It talks to you and gives you turn-by-turn directions. But there is one problem: it can give you the wrong directions and you may get lost! It is important to remember that these are not fool-proof devices.

God has given us two GPS devices. One is internal and the other is external.

> Pay close attention to these two spiritual GPS devices and you will get to the place where God wants you to be. You will accomplish the things that God wants you to accomplish.

Both of them are 100 percent accurate. The first is the GPS device of the Holy Spirit located inside of you. The Holy Spirit is always faithful, leading you where you should go and telling you what you should do, who you should date, what you should purchase, and what job you should take. However, whether you choose to obey the Holy Spirit is a different issue.

The second GPS device is the Word of God. If you listen and obey the Word of God, then you will always stay on track and will never veer off course during your journey of obedience. The Holy Spirit always bears witness to the Word, and the Word always bears witness to the Holy Spirit. They will never compete or contradict. They are synched together to provide double confirmation in your heart for what God is leading you to do. By paying close attention to these two powerful guiding forces, you will get to the place where God wants you to be, and along the way, you will accomplish the things that God wants you to accomplish.

I have a book in my office titled *The School of Obedience* by Andrew Murray. In Chapter 3, he makes a powerful statement about obedience. He says, "The secret of obedience…is the clear and close personal relationship to God. All of our attempts after full obedience will be failures until we get access to His abiding fellowship. It is God's holy presence consciously abiding with us that keeps us from disobeying him."[5] We want to ensure that our journey of obedience leads us to deliverance, maintaining our close relationship with God, and helping transform the lives of others.

ENDNOTES

1. http://www.sermonillustrations.com/a-z/o/obedience.htm. Original source unknown.

2. Thomas Kempis, *The Imitation of Christ* (New York: Doubleday, 1955).

3. Story reported by Good Morning America and ABCNews.com, June 6, 2008.

4.   Moody Bible Institute, *Today in the Word,* November, 1989, p. 11.

5.   Andrew Murray, *The School of Obedience* (Chicago: Moody Press), p. 37.

Chapter 4

Row, Row, Row Your Boat—
A Journey of Frustration

Evils in the journey of life are like the hills which alarm
travelers on their road. Both appear great at a distance,
but when we approach them we find that they are less
insurmountable than we had conceived.
—Charles Caleb Colton

A guy in Michigan walked into a fast-food restaurant and pulled a gun on the man behind the counter. He demanded that the worker give him all of the money from the register. The employee replied that he could not do that unless an order was placed and rung up on the register. The robber ordered some onion rings. The cashier then replied that they did not serve onion rings at breakfast time. The robber was so frustrated that he walked out; he was caught a few minutes later by the police.

Frustration is like mosquitoes in the summertime, being forced to watch an infomercial, or trying to figure out income tax instructions. Frustration is like spam e-mails and rising gas prices. There are many irritating frustrations throughout life. We must learn to live with frustration because it is part of the maturation process of our relationship with Christ. This statement may seem surprising to you. You, like many others, may think that when you give your life to Christ, your frustrations will disappear. It is easy to believe that everything is going to be wonderful and euphoric now that you're a believer. You may think that you will simply float through life without a care in the world because you have accepted Christ into your heart. Wrong!

THE FRUSTRATIONS OF LIFE

Even in your relationship with Christ, there will be frustrations that you will have to face. Frustrations in all aspects of life are inevitable and cannot be eliminated. However, you *can* eliminate carnal or immature responses to frustration. Everyone handles frustration differently. Some let it out through road rage or verbal attacks while others may smash their fists against the wall or throw things. Those types of actions are not mature or constructive ways to handle life's frustrations.

Even the disciples who walked and talked with Jesus were frustrated at times.

FEELING THE DISCIPLES' FRUSTRATIONS

Matthew records a journey of frustration taken by the disciples while they were ministering with Jesus. Along the way, they experienced a whole host of frustrations. Matthew 14 relays some of the journey:

> *Immediately Jesus made the disciples get into the boat and go on ahead of Him to the other side, while He dismissed the crowd. After He had dismissed them, He went up on a mountainside by Himself to pray. When evening came, He was there alone, but the boat was already a considerable distance from land, buffeted by the waves because the wind was against it. During the fourth watch of the night Jesus went out to them, walking on the lake. When the*

disciples saw Him walking on the lake, they were terrified. "It's a ghost," they said, and cried out in fear. But Jesus immediately said to them: "Take courage! It is I. Don't be afraid." "Lord, if it's You," Peter replied, "tell me to come to you on the water." "Come," He said. Then Peter got down out of the boat, walked on the water and came toward Jesus. But when he saw the wind, he was afraid and, beginning to sink, cried out, "Lord, save me!" Immediately Jesus reached out His hand and caught him. "You of little faith," He said, "why did you doubt?" And when they climbed into the boat, the wind died down (Matthew 14:22-32).

Before explaining the significance of this passage, it is important to understand what took place just prior to these events. The disciples were with Jesus as thousands of people gathered to hear Him teach. People were captivated by what He was saying. The Bible says there were 5,000 men, not counting the women and children. It can be assumed there were between 10,000 and 12,000 people gathered on the hillside (see Matt. 14:13-21). The disciples had planned to go to the village and get food for the people. They had a logical, well-thought out plan. However, Jesus had a different idea, one that would challenge their faith immensely. He looked at them and said, *"You give them something to eat"* (see Matt. 14:16).

It is easy to imagine what the disciples must have been thinking. How were they going to feed thousands and thousands of people in the middle of nowhere? Reading between the lines, Jesus' intent was to develop something that was inside of the disciples by implanting a plan that they did not understand nor did they think was going to work. Obviously, they knew that He was the Messiah, so they wanted to do what He asked even if it made no sense to them. The only food they found was that of a little boy who had five loaves of bread and two fish. It was clear the disciples lacked faith when they returned to Jesus and told Him about the little sustenance they had located.

The Lord never panics.

You must love the Lord for the fact that He never panics. He does not verbally abuse them with a tirade. Instead, Jesus thanked them, blessed the food they found, and handed it back so that they could distribute it to the people. Many familiar with this story assume that the multiplication of these little loaves and couple of fish happened at the moment when Jesus prayed over it and blessed it. Well, this is not what happened. Jesus blessed the bread and the fish and handed back the same five loaves of bread and the same two fish. Then He instructed them to distribute this food to the people. The disciples must have stood there staring at Him, wondering what they were going to do with a hungry mob of 12,000 people when all they had were a few morsels that would not have even satisfied the 12 of them. They may have thought that a riot would break out when their baskets were emptied after just a few minutes.

THE GREAT STEWARDSHIP PRINCIPLE

While the Bible does not say which disciple took the lead, it is clear that all of them followed and began handing out the food. The Bible does relate that they distributed the food to everyone so that all ate and were satisfied—and that there were 12 baskets of food leftover that they picked up afterward. The beauty of this story is that the miracle happened as they obeyed the Lord. Jesus was trying to stretch their faith. He wanted them to be not just witnesses of a miracle, but to be part of the miracle. As they stepped out and obeyed Him, the miracle occurred.

Often, we may think that when the Lord blesses us, then we will start obeying Him by tithing and giving. It does not work that way. The truth: God will not bless us or allow us to prosper until we obey Him. We may want to wait to serve Him until after that big miracle or for that lottery ticket to win. However, this is not how He operates. As we obey God in the area of stewardship, then the miracle of multiplication takes place, and the avenue opens for the blessings of God in your life. When we obey Him, God can bless us in the way that He so desires.

> As they obeyed the Lord, the miracle happened.

EXCITEMENT AND FRUSTRATION

The disciples were excited to be part of the miracle, but Jesus did not let them revel in the moment. Instead, He immediately sent them on to the next assignment. Jesus told the disciples to get into the boat and row to the other side, and He would meet them later. The disciples did not realize there was a twofold miracle that would unfold for them. They thought what happened was wonderful, but did not realize there were more amazing events to come.

While they pondered the feeding miracle, the disciples boarded the boat to cross the Sea of Galilee around six in the evening in order to reach Capernaum on the north shore. At its widest point, the Sea of Galilee is seven miles across. During the first couple of hours in the boat, they were still excited about how Jesus performed the miracle through them. Each of the disciples shared their perspective on the miracle as they rowed.

Everything was wonderful until frustration set in.

Have you ever noticed that the Lord does not give you much time to celebrate a victory before you are faced with a new set of frustrations? I have witnessed great breakthroughs, victories, and mountain top experiences, as well as frustration after His instructions to move forward.

Jesus sent the disciples to another place immediately because He did not want them to get too caught up in the moment and assume that is how all miracles occur. Our tendency is to capture and stay in the moment when God begins to move in our lives. However, the Lord does not work that way. He does not allow us to box Him in.

Four Facts about Frustration

To eliminate the carnal and immature responses to any frustration that you experience, it is important to meditate on these four facts:

1. The absence of frustration does not mean that you are in the center of God's will.

We mistakenly assume that when we are in the center of God's will we experience a peaceful existence where everything is quiet and things fall into place. The reality: when we are in the middle of the will of God, we may possibly be surrounded by frustrations. The disciples were exactly where Jesus wanted them. They were in the middle of God's will and they were obeying Him. Obedience and simply doing what He has told us to do put us in the center of His will.

If frustration is missing from your life, this may be an indication that you have chosen the path of least resistance; hence, you may be out of the will of God. I am very familiar with the incredible place of solitude and shalom that you can experience in the center of the will of God. However, I also know from experience that I can be in the middle of God's will and be at the height of frustration.

The disciples endeavored to do what Jesus asked, but frustration set in when the journey across the Sea of Galilee took longer than expected. Their shoulders ached. Calluses and blisters formed. The waves soaked them and the winds were an enemy to their progress. John 6 reads that they had gone only three miles and it was already 3 A.M. This meant that they had rowed for nine hours and still had not reached Capernaum. They started playing the blame game with each other about who was holding up the journey. They were exhausted because the wind was beating against them. Jesus was nowhere to be found, having stayed behind for private prayer with His Father.

Have you ever been at a point where you are trying to obey the Lord only to be maxed out on your frustration level, wondering why He called you to this, why it has to be so hard, and why it has to be such a struggle? Finding yourself in such a place can do a real number on your theology and faith. You have frustrations and think that you are out of the will of God. This is when you might feel like giving up, like the disciples who were stuck in the middle of the Sea of Galilee.

Arguably one of the toughest nights of my life was December 31, 1999. I felt stuck, forgotten, and abandoned by the Lord. Melanie and I were in a season of transition in our ministry, and we had great hopes that we would experience a breakthrough before the year 2000 rolled around. The wind and waves were against us, and it seemed as if Jesus was nowhere to be found. Yet, we were right in the middle of God's will for our lives. During those dark days, God taught me truths, developed my faith, and shaped my character in ways that have forever shaped who I am. Looking back on it, I wouldn't trade those times and the things God taught me for anything.

2. Jesus always knows your location.

Despite the urge to give up, the disciples realized that Jesus knew their exact location. The Bible says: *"During the fourth watch of the night Jesus went out to them, walking on the lake"* (Matt. 14:25). Jesus' heavenly GPS device tracked the disciples. Not only did He know where they were, but He also sensed when they reached the pinnacle of their frustration. He knew their breaking point—the time when they reached the end of their abilities and when they had exhausted all their resources. This was the optimum point for them to open up to learning what Jesus had to teach them.

Jesus also knows your breaking point. You might remember a coach or teacher in high school or college who pushed you until you had nothing left to give. This person tested you and the team or class like crazy. You were exhausted and had leg (or brain) cramps. Others were throwing up. Everyone was sure that the leader would know you were ready to quit. However, the person knew better than you how far you could be pushed without destruction.

Jesus does the same with us. He knows just how much He can push us, how much He can stretch us, and how much He can develop our faith without destroying us. As the Bible states:

> *No temptation has seized you except what is common to man. And God is faithful; He will not let you be tempted beyond what you can bear. But when you are tempted, He will also provide a way out so that you can stand up under it* (1 Corinthians 10:13).

The Lord knows how much we can take and He wants to take us to the end of our abilities and our resources so that we will be teachable. The Bible also says:

> *God is our refuge and strength, an ever-present help in trouble. Therefore we will not fear, though the earth give way and the mountains fall into the heart of the sea* (Psalm 46:1-2).

When you are dealing with the frustrations of life because you cannot get rid of them all, this is the time to work on eliminating your immature and carnal responses to them. When you are dealing with frustrations, remember that Jesus always knows your exact location. It may feel like He is nowhere around, but trust that He knows exactly where you are and that He knows your breaking point.

3. Frustrations will try and blind you to the reality of the Lord's presence.

"When the disciples saw Him walking on the lake, they were terrified. 'It's a ghost,' they said, and cried out in fear" (Matt. 14:26). You would think that the disciples would have recognized Jesus. It was not like they had only seen Him once or twice before, they spent days and nights with Him. But He had to identify Himself to them because they thought He was a ghost. Has Jesus ever had to do that with you? Has He had to send a signal that says, "Hey, I am the Lord"? That is what He had to do with Saul in Acts 9, and that is what He had to do with the disciples. So many times in our lives, we have reached the point where we are blinded to His presence because of being distracted by trying to deal with our frustrations.

In Matthew 14:27, we have Jesus' response. He walked up to the disciples and told them, *"Take courage. It is I. Don't be afraid."* He tells you the same thing. You may be in the midst of frustrating circumstances right now:

- You don't know how you are going to pay the bills, or you don't know how your marriage is going to work out. This is when the Lord says, *"Take courage. It is I. Don't be afraid."*

- You have looked for a job for months and have no promise of one, so the Lord tells you, *"Take courage. It is I. Don't be afraid."*

- You are trying to decide where to go to college or you must decide what you are going to do about your children, so the Lord responds, *"Take courage. It is I. Don't be afraid."*

"You don't have
to be afraid."

When Jesus told the disciples that, it was His way of showing them the previous times when He was strong and faithful in their lives. This is apparent in the following passage:

Then He got into the boat and His disciples followed Him. Without warning, a furious storm came up on the lake, so that the waves swept over the boat. But Jesus was sleeping. The disciples went and woke Him, saying, "Lord, save us! We're going to drown!" He replied, "You of little faith, why are you so afraid?" Then He got up and rebuked the winds and the waves, and it was completely calm (Matthew 8:23-26).

Jesus had startled the disciples when he walked on water toward their boat. Now He was reminding them about that time. He spoke to the wind and made everything calm, as if to say, "If I did it then, I can do it now."

Jesus does the same for you. He takes you back and reminds you of those moments when you experienced breakthrough. He reminds you of those times when you did not know how you were going to pay your bills. I had someone tell me that they gave a $10 offering and it was basically all that they had because they had been without work for so long. However, they recently received an unexpected $1,000 check in the mail that would help them stay afloat and pay their bills. God will remind you of those times and of those great moments of breakthrough. It is His way of saying, "Hey, I'm still the same. You don't have to panic. You don't have to be afraid. If I came through for you before, then I will come through for you again."

Sometimes, the frustrations of life try and blind you to His presence. It may feel like He is so far away, but He knows your exact location. Even when He does show up, you may be so frustrated that you don't recognize Him. You go to church but are so frustrated. Sitting there in frustration, you see God touching people all around and watch them enter into the presence of the Lord. At the same time, you may feel cold and apathetic, thinking that God cannot move you. To you He is nowhere to be found and, because of the frustrations, you may mistakenly believe that you are not even on His radar screen anymore.

4. You conquer frustration when you fix your eyes on His face.

The Bible relates the next event by the disciples when it says, *"'Lord, if it's you,' Peter replied, 'tell me to come to you on the water'"* (Matt. 14:28). The natural tendency for the majority of the disciples was to think that Jesus would come to them, get into the boat, and everything would be OK. But Peter wanted to walk to Jesus. He went beyond expecting Jesus to operate in the same way, in the same manner, and expected something different.

If we handle frustration with a mature and faith-filled attitude, the frustrations in our lives move us out of the realm of the natural and into the realm of the supernatural. Because Peter decided that he was tired of rowing the boat and all of the frustration of not reaching the shore, he asked to come to Jesus rather than wait for Jesus to get into the boat.

Many times we want Jesus to get in the middle of what we are involved in, but He is waiting for us to come to Him. This is not because He is arrogant and wants everyone else to make the first move. Instead, Jesus wants to move us out of the realm of the natural and into the realm of the supernatural.

Peter asked Jesus basically if he should leave the realm of the natural and move into this realm of the supernatural by coming to Him. Jesus' reply is one word: "Come." An invitation was extended to all 12 disciples to leave the place of frustration by moving from the realm of the natural into the realm of the supernatural. He was basically telling them that He knew that they were all in the same boat or similar circumstances, and there was much more that they could experience if they would just take that first step out.

Then Jesus called them to the second part of the twofold miracle. He told them that He knew that they could live within that realm of the supernatural. However, it was only Peter who had the guts to swing his legs over the side of the boat. He started walking on the water toward Jesus. His eyes were fixed on Jesus. As the Protector, Peter recognized Him. As the Deliverer, he recognized Him as the One who could bring an end to the frustration. However, the Bible says that when Peter saw the wind—the source of the frustration—he made the mistake of glancing away from the Lord's eyes for an instant, and the frustration returned.

Again, we tend to do the same thing. At first we get caught up in the presence of God and fix our eyes on Him. We choose to operate in faith and stop listening to the lies of the enemy. However, when we take our eyes off of Him, we quickly slide back into facing the same set of frustrations and circumstances, becoming momentarily distracted by them.

As soon as Peter looked away, the Bible says he began to sink. Peter moved away from the realm of the supernatural back into the realm of the natural because his eyes were not on Jesus. Before that, however, he defied the laws of gravity by walking on the water. As Peter started to sink, he cried out to the Lord to save him. Immediately, Jesus reached out His hand. Jesus didn't reach out to Peter after he had sunk under the water two or three times. He didn't allow him to sink so as to drive the point home about never losing his focus again. No. Jesus is so full of grace and mercy that He immediately reached out His hand.

It is easy to imagine the look of panic on Peter's face and the terror in his eyes as the water came up around him. But Jesus brought peace to Peter and looked at him as a father would his son when he wants him to know how proud he is for having the guts to try something. Jesus took his hand and they boarded the boat together.

If we handle frustrations with immature and carnal responses, we will be anchored to the realm of the natural. However, if we choose to respond to the frustrations of life in ways that please the Lord, we will be propelled out of the realm of the natural and into the supernatural realm where God is waiting for us.

QUESTION YOUR FRUSTRATIONS

If you are at the height of your frustration level, ask yourself the following questions:

1. Have I obeyed God, or has disobedience produced frustration in me?

You can obey God and still find yourself right in the middle of frustrating circumstances, just like the disciples. When you obey God and find yourself dealing with frustrations, is your tendency to question whether you have heard from Him? Other times, when you disobey God your disobedience is what produces the frustration.

If you are at the height of frustration, you have to discern that between the two circumstances. Ask yourself: *Did I obey God? Did I do what He asked me to do?* If so and you are dealing with frustration, then you should stay faithful. Keep your eyes fixed on Him. Do not take your hands off the oars that steer you along on life's journey. If disobedience has put you in the midst of frustrations, then allow it to be an opportunity for you to repent. Proclaim out loud: "God forgive me, I blew it." Maybe it is your disobedience that is causing you not to progress. If this is the

> Many times we want Jesus to get in the middle of what we are involved in, but He is waiting for us to come to Him.

case, then you need to correct your behavior. Look to God and He will help you.

2. Do I really believe that He will never leave me and that I am on His radar screen right now?

Do I really believe that He knows my breaking point and that He will not allow me to be tested beyond what I am capable of withstanding?

3. Have I allowed my frustrations to blind me to the reality of His presence? In other words, do I even recognize Him?

It could be that you have become so focused on your frustration that you do not even recognize or know God anymore. You may not even be able to know Him if He showed up on your doorstep tomorrow because you are so blind to the reality that He is actually with you right now.

4. Have I focused more on the frustrations or more on His face?

Many times we focus on the negative—the bills, relationships, the harassing boss, the kids who have strayed away from God—and on all of the other stuff that can consume our minds rather than focusing on the Lord's face. When you focus on His face, you will conquer frustration.

The Lord wants you to experience peace even in the midst of frustration. Come to God, focus intently on His face, enter the realm of the supernatural, and experience freedom from the chains of frustration.

Chapter 5

Gettin' Your Praise On—
A Journey Of Exaltation

We are not human beings on a spiritual journey. We are spiritual beings on a human journey.
—Steven Covey

Then Nebuchadnezzar said, "Praise be to the God of Shadrach, Meshach and Abednego, who has sent his angel and rescued his servants! They trusted in Him and defied the king's command and were willing to give up their lives rather than serve or worship any god except their own God." (Daniel 3:28).

THE word *exalt* is not a word we use much today. Not many of us, when we greet each other, say, "Hey there, I exalt you," or "Nice to meet you, I exalt you." Although it is not a common word in today's society, it is important to understand the concept of exaltation because, depending on what version of the Bible you prefer, you will find the word *exalt* used about 100 times. For instance, in the New International Version of the Bible, exalt is used 97 times. Here are a few examples:

Glorify the Lord with me; let us exalt his name together (Psalm 34:3).

Be exalted, O God, above the heavens; let your glory be over all the earth (Psalm 57:5).

For you, O Lord, are the Most High over all the earth; you are exalted far above all gods (Psalm 97:9).

Exalt the Lord our God and worship at his footstool; he is holy (Psalm 99:5).

The dictionary defines *exalt* as to hold something or someone in very high regard. Exalt also means to speak or think highly of that person. The second part of that definition involves raising someone to a higher rank or position of higher power. The word *exalt* has particular importance for three men who took a journey of exaltation as seen in the Book of Daniel.

TRAVELING WITH SHADRACH, MESHACH, AND ABEDNEGO

In traveling with Shadrach, Meshach, and Abednego on the journey of exaltation, you will discover some common threads that will help you to exalt the Lord throughout your life.

The story begins in Daniel 1. The Babylonians have invaded Israel and have held them captive for 70 years. The ruler of the Babylonians, King Nebuchadnezzar, begins handpicking young men for service in his royal court. He selects Daniel as well as Shadrach, Meshach, and Abednego. They are described as:

young men without any physical defect, handsome, show-ing aptitude for every kind of learning, well informed, quick to understand, and qualified to serve in the king's palace... (Daniel 1:4).

These young men are heads above others and considered the cream of the crop:

In every matter of wisdom and understanding about which the king questioned them, he found them ten times better than all the magicians and enchanters in his whole kingdom (Daniel 1:20).

The second chapter of Daniel focuses on the dreams of Nebuchadnezzar. The king is troubled because he cannot find anyone in the land who can interpret his dreams. However, he learns that Daniel is a God-fearing Jewish man who, prophetically, has the ability to tap into the voice of God and discern dreams. The king approaches Daniel and shares his dreams with him. Daniel immediately tells him the meanings of the dreams. As a result, Daniel wins great favor with King Nebuchadnezzar and is elevated to a high position, prime minister of the entire Babylonian empire. At Daniel's urging, Shadrach, Meshach, and Abednego become the administrators over the province of Babylon.

The action really picks up in the third chapter of Daniel, when King Nebuchadnezzar decides that he wants everybody in the land to worship him. Obviously, there is an ego problem and an arrogance that has developed in the king. He builds a 90-foot tall golden statue and declares that everybody will worship this image (see Daniel 3:1-5).

When you are a stranger in a foreign land, there may come a point when your values and beliefs will collide with those of the land. This happens to Shadrach, Meshach, and Abednego when they refuse to bow to the idol. Worshiping a human being would compromise their

> *...showing aptitude for every kind of learning, well informed, quick to understand...*

belief that God is the only One whom they should worship. King Nebuchadnezzar is furious with them but gives them a second chance. They refuse again to bow, so he throws them into a fiery furnace.

However, the Lord intervenes and saves them.

JOURNEY OF EXALTATION ENCOUNTERS

There are a number of things that you may encounter on your journey of exaltation that were first experienced by Shadrach, Meshach, and Abednego. Learning about these situations and how these faithful young men responded to them can assist you in exalting the Lord in your own life.

An Unspiritual Anthem

The concept of an unspiritual anthem appears in Daniel 3:

> *King Nebuchadnezzar made an image of gold, ninety feet high and nine feet wide, and set it up on the plain of Dura in the province of Babylon. He then summoned the satraps, prefects, governors, advisers, treasurers, judges, magistrates and all the other provincial officials to come to the dedication of the image he had set up. So the satraps, prefects, governors, advisers, treasurers, judges, magistrates and all the other provincial officials assembled for the dedication of the image that King Nebuchadnezzar had set up, and they stood before it. Then the herald loudly proclaimed, "This is what you are commanded to do, O peoples, nations and men of every language: As soon as you hear the sound of the horn, flute, zither, lyre, harp, pipes and all kinds of music, you must fall down and worship the image of gold that King Nebuchadnezzar has set*

up. Whoever does not fall down and worship will immedi-
ately be thrown into a blazing furnace." Therefore, as soon
as they heard the sound of the horn, flute, zither, lyre, harp
and all kinds of music, all the peoples, nations and men of
every language fell down and worshiped the image of gold
that King Nebuchadnezzar had set up (Daniel 3:1-7).

There is an *unspiritual anthem* that is released through the order to fall down and worship the statue. In examining this concept, there are some common elements to what is found in Heaven. In Heaven, there is a king, music like we have never heard before, and people of every nation, language, tribe. King Nebuchadnezzar's representation is a perverted picture of Heaven and a counterfeit of the real thing.

The world will always have a counterfeit replacement for the real thing. There is a sound that is being released from the earth that is intent on luring people away from the true worship of the true king and it coerces everyone to settle for a counterfeit version. Notice the role that music plays in this Scripture passage; when the music plays, everyone bows down and worships the golden image. A similar sound is being released from the earth today. The current music industry plays a key role in dumbing us down and getting us to settle for counterfeit worship rather than the authentic worship of the true King.

The truth: Everybody exalts somebody. There is someone in your life whom you have raised to a higher rank, position, and power in your life than should be. The question: who is that person in your life? You encounter unspiritual anthems every day that leads you away from the true worship of the true King. If you learn how not to be moved from this earthly sound of unholy music, you will not fall prey to counterfeit worship.

An Unwavering Allegiance

Despite this unspiritual anthem, Shadrach, Meshach, and Abednego had an unwavering allegiance. Daniel 3 explains:

At this time some astrologers came forward and denounced the Jews. They said to King Nebuchadnezzar, "O king, live forever! You have issued a decree, O king, that everyone who hears the sound of the horn, flute, zither, lyre, harp, pipes and all kinds of music must fall down and worship the image of gold, and that whoever does not fall down and worship will be thrown into a blazing furnace. But there are some Jews whom you have set over the affairs of the province of Babylon—Shadrach, Meshach and Abednego—who pay no attention to you, O king. They neither serve your gods nor worship the image of gold you have set up." Furious with rage, Nebuchadnezzar summoned Shadrach, Meshach and Abednego. So these men were brought before the king, and Nebuchadnezzar said to them, "Is it true, Shadrach, Meshach and Abednego, that you do not serve my gods or worship the image of gold I have set up? Now when you hear the sound of the horn, flute, zither, lyre, harp, pipes and all kinds of music, if you are ready to fall down and worship the image I made, very good. But if you do not worship it, you will be thrown immediately into a blazing furnace. Then what god will be able to rescue you from my hand?" Shadrach, Meshach and Abednego replied to the king, "O Nebuchadnezzar, we do not need to defend ourselves before you in this matter. If we are thrown into the blazing furnace, the God we serve is able to save us from it, and he will rescue us from your hand, O king. But even if he does not, we want you to know, O king, that we will not serve your gods or worship the image of gold you have set up" (Daniel 3:8-18).

The world will always give you plenty of opportunities to move into false worship. That is why, in terms of this unwavering allegiance, we have to understand what happens in Joshua 24:

> *Now fear the Lord and serve Him with all faithfulness. Throw away the gods your forefathers worshiped beyond the River and in Egypt, and serve the Lord. But if serving the Lord seems undesirable to you, then choose for yourselves this day whom you will serve, whether the gods your forefathers served beyond the River, or the gods of the Amorites, in whose land you are living. But as for me and my household, we will serve the Lord." Then the people answered, "Far be it from us to forsake the Lord to serve other gods!"* (Joshua 24:14-16)

The dividing line has never been clearer than now. The heat is on—just as it was for Shadrach, Meshach, and Abednego—and you must make up your mind. Where do you stand? When some are bowing their knees or sleeping around, or when others are stealing from their employer, experimenting with a homosexual lifestyle, or giving in to drinking and partying, you have got to make a decision. Where do you stand? Who will you worship? Do not play the game. Do not waffle back and forth. You cannot do one thing when you are with your friends and then act another way when you walk into church. Make up your mind. Are you going to worship Him? Are you going to serve Him? Are you just going to play it safe the rest of your life?

In these last days, you need to have an unwavering allegiance so that regardless of what anyone says or does, you show by your actions that you will not bow your knee to anything or anyone except Yahweh. There may be times when you don't feel like following through on that commitment, but you have to make up your mind on a daily basis not to put anyone or anything above God. Regardless of the fact that you may be physically sick, tired, or discouraged, if you have bills piling up, or if you are at odds with someone close, you need to decide that none of those things are going to separate you from Him. Those who possess an unwavering allegiance make the decision to keep the Lord first in their lives.

My family recently found ourselves in a challenging and painful place brought on by a season of rebellion from our daughter. I wanted to run, hide, and quit. I found myself angry and disoriented, much like the disciples in John 6. Many disciples were choosing to walk away from Jesus. He turns to the 12 to ask if they were going to abandon Him, too. Their response in verse 68 expresses how I also felt: "Lord, to whom shall we go? You have the words of eternal life." I chose to run, and ran straight into His arms through the avenue of worship. I didn't feel like worshiping, but made the choice to do so.

You may know yourself well enough to realize that if you wait until you *feel* like making the commitment, then there will be times when you will be waiting too long. Go after God. Worship Him regardless of how you feel because He deserves it. He is worthy of your praise and your mind should be made up. In Joshua 24:15, Joshua told the Israelites that they had to make up their mind. They were living in the land of the Amorites, and there were the gods that the Amorites worshiped and there was the one true God. The Israelites had a serious decision to make.

Like the Israelites, you have to decide—the Bible says to decide today. Choose right now who you will worship and serve. If you don't make up your mind right now, it will be a lot tougher for you to take a stand when you get into the midst of the crowd and everyone else is bowing. That is why unwavering allegiance is so important. There is only One to whom you should bow your knee to, raise to a higher rank, and position as a greater power. It is not a pop star, athlete, the economy, money, a house, a boat, or recreation. It is Yahweh. He is the one true God—the one who should receive the best of your worship.

Uncontrollable Anger

There are situations involving uncontrollable anger that you may encounter on your journey of exaltation. The three faithful Hebrews witnessed the uncontrollable anger of King Nebuchadnezzar:

> *Then Nebuchadnezzar was furious with Shadrach, Meshach and Abednego, and his attitude toward them changed. He ordered the furnace heated seven times hotter than usual and commanded some of the strongest soldiers in his army to tie up Shadrach, Meshach and Abednego and throw them into the blazing furnace. So these men, wearing their robes, trousers, turbans and other clothes, were bound and thrown into the blazing furnace. The king's command was so urgent and the furnace so hot that the flames of the fire killed the soldiers who took up Shadrach, Meshach and Abednego, and these three men, firmly tied, fell into the blazing furnace* (Daniel 3:19-23).

When you decide that you are going to stand in allegiance for the Lord, there are people in the world whose attitude will change toward you. Nebuchadnezzar represents satan in the Scriptures. Babylon is the Old Testament picture of the world's system, with Nebuchadnezzar as the ruler. When you choose to stand for the Lord, there is an enemy who becomes furious. If you are not living for the Lord, then you are no threat to the devil. He does not need to mess with you.

However, when you make up your mind and resolve in your heart that you are going to bow your knee to Yahweh, the enemy becomes furious toward you. Even people around you may not respect or understand your stand. This may cause their attitude toward you to change. There is hostility rising in society against those who stand for Christ. At many workplaces, it is not acceptable to have religious symbols on your desk—or even on your lawn at home. It is not politically correct to wish someone Merry Christmas. Instead, we are supposed to say Happy Holidays.

Why? Because of the rising level of anger and hostility toward those who commit to the one true God. People do not know how to be mad at God because they cannot see Him, so they direct their anger toward believers because they can see us and we are accessible.

There was a woman who worked for British Airways for several years. She was a very good employee and participated in the diversity training offered by the airline for all their employees. Right after the training, the airline suspended her because she refused to take the cross off her necklace while working. At the same time, though, Muslim employees were allowed to wear turbans and Sikhs could wear their iron bangles. Yet, this Christian woman could not wear her cross necklace. Why? Because of the anger in the earth that says, "We do not respect the stand that you have taken for the Lord. We are going to do everything we can to cause you to compromise and settle for a counterfeit experience."

Some people get angry with you because they have never seen the same level of courage in themselves that you possess. Other people are angry with you because they have been blinded by the god of this age. The Bible says, *"Blessed are those who are persecuted because of righteousness, for theirs is the kingdom of heaven"* (Matt. 5:10). The Scriptures also exclaim, *"Rejoice and be glad, because great is your reward in heaven, for in the same way they persecuted the prophets who were before you"* (Matt. 5:12). Blessed are you when people curse you and falsely accuse you of all kinds of things because of the Lord. When there is this hostility and uncontrollable anger because people do not respect the stand that you have taken, the Bible says to rejoice and be glad because your inheritance is the kingdom of Heaven.

An Unnatural Addition

The Bible explains the concept of an unnatural addition as part of the story of Shadrach, Meshach, and Abednego:

Then King Nebuchadnezzar leaped to his feet in amazement and asked his advisers, "Weren't there three men that we tied up and threw into the fire?" They replied, "Certainly, O king." He said, "Look! I see four men walking around in the fire, unbound and unharmed, and the fourth looks like a son of the gods." Nebuchadnezzar then approached the opening of the blazing furnace and shouted, "Shadrach, Meshach and Abednego, servants of the Most High God, come out! Come here!" So Shadrach, Meshach and Abednego came out of the fire, and the satraps, prefects, governors and royal advisers crowded around them. They saw that the fire had not harmed their bodies, nor was a hair of their heads singed; their robes were not scorched, and there was no smell of fire on them (Daniel 3:24-27).

Because we live in this natural realm, we are subject to the laws of nature, which put restrictions on our lives. If we go against these laws of nature, then we will suffer the consequences. Think about the law of gravity or the law of inertia. If we try and go against these laws, we will suffer the consequences.

We are restricted by the laws of nature, but so often we have allowed the laws of this natural world to overshadow the laws of the supernatural world. We do not see and experience the miracles that we read about in Scripture and that we have heard about happening in generations past, because we have allowed ourselves to become restricted and imprisoned by the laws of nature.

We have allowed the realm of the natural to overcome the realm of the supernatural. We forget that we serve a God who is not bound or restricted by the laws of nature. He created the laws of nature, so He can supersede them. That is why He could walk on water; raise people from the dead; cause the wind to calm and the sun to stand still. It makes sense that when Jesus taught the disciples to pray He knew they were praying to a God who is in the realm of the supernatural and He said:

You have to factor a supernatural God into your natural equation.

This, then, is how you should pray: "Our Father in heaven, hallowed be Your name, Your kingdom come, Your will be done on earth as it is in heaven..." (Matthew 6:9-10).

Although we are restricted by the realm of nature, we do not have to be prisoners of it. We can tap into His supernatural realm and say, "God, bring Your realm and overshadow this realm so that while we are restricted by the laws of nature, we serve a God who is above them." In this way, we do not have to be slaves and prisoners of the laws of nature.

On their journey of exaltation, Shadrach, Meshach, and Abednego realize that *you have to factor a supernatural God into your natural equation.* I believe that Shadrach, Meshach, and Abednego decided that if they were going to be thrown into a blazing furnace, then the God they serve would save them from it. In other words, they know the laws of nature mean that they would be burned—but they factor a supernatural God into the realm of the natural. Because they serve God who is above the laws of nature, He can rescue them from the blazing furnace.

In your own journey of exaltation, you have to learn to factor a supernatural God into the natural equation. So while you are restricted by the laws of nature, you will not be a prisoner of the natural realm because your citizenship is not on this earth. Your citizenship is in Heaven, and you can bring that Kingdom into this realm.

They trust God. Obviously as devout young Jewish men, Shadrach, Meshach, and Abednego are familiar with the writings of Isaiah, the prophet, who wrote:

> *But now, this is what the Lord says—He who created you, O Jacob, He who formed you, O Israel: "Fear not, for I have redeemed you; I have summoned you by name; you are*

Mine. When you pass through the waters, I will be with you; and when you pass through the rivers, they will not sweep over you. When you walk through the fire, you will not be burned; the flames will not set you ablaze. For I am the Lord, your God, the Holy One of Israel, your Savior; I give Egypt for your ransom, Cush and Seba in your stead" (Isaiah 43:1-3).

Shadrach, Meshach, and Abednego say they are going to trust God because their forefather, Isaiah, wrote that when we touch fire and when we walk through the natural realm of water or rivers, they will not harm or overtake us because the Lord has redeemed us. He has called us by name and we belong to Him. These three trust that He will do that for them. They also trust His heart and His plan for their lives. They say in Daniel 3:17: *"Our God will deliver us."* That is the key. However, in Daniel 3:18, they make one of the greatest statements of faith in the entire Bible: *"But even if He does not, we want you to know, O king that we will not serve your gods or worship the image of gold you have set up."*

These young men are not waffling in their faith. Instead, they recognize He is able and they understand that His ways are higher than human ways. There are times when we do not understand the way God works, but when we cannot trace His hand, we should still trust His heart. We will factor Him into the natural equation and we will leave the results up to Him. This is because we trust that He has a plan for our lives, and that He will carry it out if we are faithful to Him.

The unspiritual anthem that rises from the earth has to be met with unwavering allegiance. Some people will change in their attitude toward you. They will unleash an uncontrollable anger toward you because they do not respect the stand that you have taken. However, you will endure because you have factored in your supernatural God into the natural equation.

AN UNEXPECTED SPIRITUAL AWAKENING

The result of the first four experiences leads to the fifth one—an unexpected awakening. This last experience provides the reason why we should go through the other experiences in order to arrive at this destination. The Bible says:

> Then Nebuchadnezzar said, "Praise be to the God of Shadrach, Meshach and Abednego, who has sent His angel and rescued His servants! They trusted in Him and defied the king's command and were willing to give up their lives rather than serve or worship any god except their own God. Therefore, I decree that the people of any nation or language who say anything against the God of Shadrach, Meshach and Abednego be cut into pieces and their houses be turned into piles of rubble, for no other god can save in this way" (Daniel 3:28-29).

Your journey of exaltation can lead to a spiritual awakening in people around you. As they watch you take this journey—and, believe me, they are watching—it can have a positive effect on many of them. Your journey can cause them to see that they have been settling for a counterfeit worship of manmade gods or even themselves. Those watching you will recognize that what you have is the real deal, an authentic worship of the true God, and they will want the same.

This experience happened in Acts 16. Paul and Silas had been arrested and thrown into a cold, damp, dark, smelly, and rat-infested Roman dungeon. They had been flogged and were chained to the wall:

> About midnight Paul and Silas were praying and singing hymns to God, and the other prisoners were listening to them. Suddenly there was such a violent earthquake that the foundations of the prison were shaken. At once all the prison doors flew open, and everybody's chains came loose.

> *The jailer woke up, and when he saw the prison doors open, he drew his sword and was about to kill himself because he thought the prisoners had escaped. But Paul shouted, "Don't harm yourself! We are all here!" The jailer called for lights, rushed in and fell trembling before Paul and Silas. He then brought them out and asked, "Sirs, what must I do to be saved?"* (Acts 16:25-30)

This Scripture explains the unexpected awakening on the part of the jailer due to the faithfulness of Paul and Silas. The experience continues:

> *They replied, "Believe in the Lord Jesus, and you will be saved—you and your household." Then they spoke the word of the Lord to him and to all the others in his house. At that hour of the night the jailer took them and washed their wounds; then immediately he and all his family were baptized. The jailer brought them into his house and set a meal before them; he was filled with joy because he had come to believe in God—he and his whole family* (Acts 16:31-34).

An unexpected awakening happens when you stand when everyone else bows. Taking a stand says you have made up your mind and you know who you are going to worship. Your heart is not divided and you are not a double-minded person. You are committed to the decision that you have reserved your best affection and worship for Him and Him alone. Regardless of what anybody else does or says, you choose to worship and exalt Yahweh.

Chapter 6

Simple Is Good—A Journey of Survival

The journey is the reward.
—Taoist saying

I N his classic manner and well-known voice, radio show host Paul Harvey told the story of how an old man with gray hair, stooped over and frail, would walk out onto a dilapidated pier on the east coast of Florida, carrying a bucket full of shrimp. About sunset, he would go to the pier and feed the seagulls, who would know to watch for him. It was his way of thanking the seagulls for helping him survive. He did this every Friday night up until 1973, the year he died. Thirty-five years earlier, as a young and vibrant man, he had served as the captain of a B17 airplane during World War II. His name was Captain Eddie Rickenbacker, and he had been entrusted with an important message to carry to General Douglas MacArthur.

Captain Rickenbacker and his crew were flying over the South Pacific when something went wrong with the mission and they found themselves out of radio contact and running low on fuel. Captain Rickenbacker ditched the plane in the South Pacific and, for the next month, he and his men battled the scorching heat and weather, and one of the great enemies, starvation.

They were in a 9 foot by 5 foot lifeboat. Sharks larger than their life-boat continued to bump against the boat and threaten them. After nearly eight days, they ran out of food. Some of the rations had been eaten, others had been destroyed by the saltwater. Captain Rickenbacker recalled that hot afternoon when William Cherry, one of the crew, led devotions for the men. They knew that without a miracle they would all die. They prayed and sang songs together. There was a little bit of conversation, but it quickly died because everyone was so famished and weak.

Captain Rickenbacker lowered his hat over his eyes to protect his face from the scorching sun and soon fell asleep. Captain Rickenbacker said that, while he was asleep, he felt something land on his head. He knew, without being able to see, that it was a seagull. He peered out from underneath his hat and saw the faces of the other men in the lifeboat. They all knew that if they could catch the seagull that it might save their lives. Uncharacteristically, this seagull was hundreds of miles from land. The rest, they say, was history, as Captain Eddie Rickenbacker managed to catch the seagull. They ate the flesh of the seagull and used the intestines to fish and catch other food. They all survived but one after 22 days adrift. So every Friday night, Captain Rickenbacker would walk out onto the pier with a bucket of shrimp and feed the seagulls as a thank you.[1]

In our journey in life, we quickly discover that we will face some challenges that will seek to destroy us. In Acts 27, there is a graphic description of just such an encounter and such a storm. Going back a couple of chapters, the Scriptures relate that Paul had been arrested. He had been preaching the gospel and the religious people were sick of him stirring up controversy, so they arrested him and falsely accused him of things that could not be proven.

In Acts 26, it says that Paul was passed from ruler to ruler because nobody knew what to do with him. They could not figure out what wrong he had committed. Paul made his appeal to Caesar and he was sent to Agrippa who said, "I can't find anything that he has done wrong. I don't see any reason why he should be put in chains and I certainly don't see any reason why he should be put to death. But because he has appealed to Caesar, he has to be sent to Rome." Agrippa even said that, had he not appealed to Caesar, he could have released him. Acts 27 says:

> *When it was decided that we would sail for Italy, Paul and some other prisoners were handed over to a centurion named Julius, who belonged to the Imperial Regiment. We boarded a ship from Adramyttium about to sail for ports along the coast of the province of Asia, and we put out to sea. Aristarchus, a Macedonian from Thessalonica, was with us. The next day we landed at Sidon; and Julius, in kindness to Paul, allowed him to go to his friends so they might provide for his needs. From there we put out to sea again and passed to the lee of Cyprus because the winds were against us. When we had sailed across the open sea off the coast of Cilicia and Pamphylia, we landed at Myra in Lycia. There the centurion found an Alexandrian ship sailing for Italy and put us on board. We made slow headway for many days and had difficulty arriving off Cnidus. When the wind did not allow us to hold our course, we sailed to the lee of Crete, opposite Salmone. We moved along the coast with difficulty and came to a place called Fair Havens, near the town of Lasea (Acts 27:1-8).*

Now this is where the story gets really good. Let's examine some of what occurred in Acts 27 to gain some practical wisdom of survival that can be applied to our lives. We all face storms. We all walk through difficult places. From the remaining verses in Acts 27, are seven steps for surviving the storms of life:

1. Choose logos over logic.

> *Much time had been lost, and sailing had already become dangerous because by now it was after the Fast, so Paul*

> God gives you the ability to think and reason, but you have to allow faith to be the ultimate deciding factor in your life.

warned them, "Men, I can see that our voyage is going to be disastrous and bring great loss to ship and cargo, and to our own lives also." But the centurion, instead of listening to what Paul said, followed the advice of the pilot and of the owner of the ship. Since the harbor was unsuitable to winter in, the majority decided that we should sail on, hoping to reach Phoenix and winter there. This was a harbor in Crete, facing both southwest and northwest (Acts 27:9-12).

God gives us the ability to reason and think through decisions as well as to logically make decisions. Those are gifts from the Lord. However, the Christian journey also involves faith. If you are allowing reason and logic to overshadow faith, then you are walking by sight and not by faith. If you are always leaning toward reason, then you are walking according to the things that you know and that you can figure out. In other words, you trust your own wisdom above that of the Lord. God gives us the ability to think and reason, but we have to factor in faith and allow it to be the ultimate deciding factor in our lives.

The word *logos* is a Greek word defined as "related to speech, a word uttered by a living voice, embodies a concept or an idea, what someone has said; more specifically, a word, the sayings of God, a decree, a mandate, or an order."[2] Logos simply means the spoken word of the Lord. If you are going to survive the storms of life, then you have to choose the word of the Lord over logic and your own ability to reason.

That is the mistake made aboard the ship, as seen in Acts 27:11-12. Paul had a logos word from God. He told them that their voyage was going to be disastrous to the cargo as well as to their own lives and that they should not continue. However, the Bible says that the centurion trusted the advice of the pilot and the owner of the ship. That was the logical decision because he assumes that those guys—the pilot and the owner of the ship—are knowledgeable sailors. It was a dangerous time to be sailing.

Paul had a word from the Lord and he shared it with them, but the majority decided to sail on. The majority, oftentimes, will go against the Word of the Lord. Because of this, you must choose logos—the Word of God, the spoken Word of the Lord—over logic. Doing so involves discerning the voice of God and knowing His voice before you get into the midst of the storm. If you wait until you are in the midst of the storm, then it might be too late as the winds are howling and the waves are bashing against the side of your boat of life. In all the chaos, you may have difficulty discerning the voice of the Lord. The time to choose the voice of God over logic is *before* you sail into the midst of the storm.

Here's the thing: Sometimes things just do not make sense to us. The Lord will speak a word to us. We feel this inclination from the Holy Spirit that we should do one thing and it totally goes against logic and reason. It can be difficult to choose the logos Word of the Lord over logic and reason because it just doesn't make sense. If you want to survive the storms of life, then it is absolutely necessary that you select the spoken Word of the Lord over logic and reason.

2. Drop anchor and ride it out.

When a gentle south wind began to blow, they thought they had obtained what they wanted; so they weighed anchor and sailed along the shore of Crete. Before very long, a wind of hurricane force, called the "northeaster," swept down from the island. The ship was caught by the storm and could not head into the wind; so we gave way to it and were driven along. As we passed to the lee of a small island called Cauda, we were hardly able to make the lifeboat secure. When the men had hoisted it aboard, they passed ropes under the ship itself to hold it together. Fearing that they would run aground on the sandbars of Syrtis, they lowered the sea anchor and let the ship be driven along (Acts 27:13-17).

Without an anchor, a ship is in serious danger of running aground. Likewise, a life without an anchor is in jeopardy of being destroyed. We must have an anchor, because when the winds begin to push us in a direction that we do not want to go or when the waves are threatening to push us against the rocks, we need to be able to drop anchor to deter disaster. An anchor slows our pace when the winds and storms of life seek to shove us against the rocks and destroy us. If the ship is faith, then the anchor is the Word of God.

So God has given both His promise and His oath. These two things are unchangeable because it is impossible for God to lie. Therefore, we who have fled to Him for refuge can have great confidence as we hold to the hope that lies before us. This hope is a strong and trustworthy anchor for our souls. It leads us through the curtain into God's inner sanctuary (Hebrews 6:18-19 NLT).

When you are caught in the storms of life, you have to find something to anchor your life to that will slow your pace and keep you from disaster—the Word of God is the best anchor. But oftentimes people find the wrong thing to use as an anchor. They think that they are secure but then find that their family has been dashed against the rocks. Their finances have come to ruin. Their relationships, children, business, or even their walk with the Lord has shipwrecked because the thing that they thought would bring security actually causes their destruction.

When we are in the midst of the storm, we have to have a secure anchor. The Book of Hebrews tells us that God has given us His oath and His promise and that this combination is a trustworthy anchor for our souls. If we depend on the Word of God, it will lead us through the curtain and into God's inner sanctuary. In other words, in the midst of the storm, you can find a peace that surpasses all understanding. How? Because this peace comes through the Word of God.

You may have been in the midst of a storm with churning waves and raging wind, but somehow through logos, the Word of God, you have found a place where you can lay down and sleep at night. You can smile throughout the day although it makes no sense. This is a peace on the inside within your soul that surpasses all understanding.

In my lifetime, I have spent only one night in a hospital due to illness. I had experienced some strange stomach pains along with fever on a few occasions in 1998. However, what happened on a November Friday morning that year was different. I was awakened very early with sharp, severe pains beyond anything I had experienced before. My wife was at a conference in Florida, and I was alone with, at that time, our only child. In spite of the debilitating pain, I somehow managed to drive to the ER. After running numerous tests, the attending physician came into the room, looked me straight in the eyes, and announced, "You have a life-threatening illness!" His statement was shocking to say the least. But a peace arose in my soul that refused to agree with the diagnosis. The storm was raging all around, yet I was experiencing a supernatural peace! And 36 hours later, I walked out of the hospital, leaving behind doctors, X-rays, and reports that could find nothing wrong.

3. Simplify.

We took such a violent battering from the storm that the next day they began to throw the cargo overboard. On the third day, they threw the ship's tackle overboard with their own hands (Acts 27:18-19).

There are times in life when you just have to strip down to the bare necessities in order to survive. That is God's plan in your life. He wants you to get rid of cargo that He never intended for you to carry. However, there are people walking around with extra baggage that was once very precious to them but now it just holds them back. Some things that were so valuable were only luxuries not necessary for survival. When you simplify your life, you discover things about the Lord that you might have forgotten, as well as learn things about yourself that help you survive.

At this point in the story, those onboard with Paul are throwing cargo overboard in the midst of the storm to lighten the load. This is something that Jesus does masterfully in our lives. He is a sterling example of someone who understood the simple life. Jesus knew simplicity. He lived during a point in history when the landscape of religion had become so complicated that people constantly debated about the most important commandments of the Scriptures. In fact, the Jews had 613 laws that they had to abide by. Imagine that![3]

There were scholars and Jewish leaders who spent all of their time debating how the laws should be grouped, how they should be classified, and which ones were the most important. They came up with 248 affirmative "thou shall" laws, which corresponded to the number of parts in the body. They created 365 negative "thou shall not" laws that corresponded to the number of days in the year, totaling 613 laws that the Jews were expected to obey and follow. Jesus was living in the middle of this complexity. Yet He knew how to simplify things. Matthew 22 relates how the Sadducees tried to trap Jesus by asking Him a question about marriage in Heaven. Matthew 22:34 says, *"Hearing that Jesus had silenced the Sadducees, the Pharisees got together."*

The Pharisees wanted to discredit Jesus.

> *One of them, an expert in the law, tested him with this question: "Teacher, which is the greatest commandment in the Law?" Jesus replied: "'Love the Lord your God with all your heart and with all your soul and with all your*

mind.' This is the first and greatest commandment. And the second is like it: 'Love your neighbor as yourself.' All the Law and the Prophets hang on these two commandments" (Matthew 22:35-40).

That was a tough question as none of them had come up with an answer after debating over the 613 laws. Jesus takes 613 laws and sums them up in two statements. How could He do that? He understands simplicity. In Matthew 11, Jesus says:

Come to me, all you who are weary and burdened, and I will give you rest. Take My yoke upon you and learn from Me, for I am gentle and humble in heart, and you will find rest for your souls. For My yoke is easy and My burden is light (Matthew 11:28-30).

According to Jewish culture, every Jewish rabbi had a set of instructions that was known as a yoke and those Jewish rabbis would cast that yoke on people. It was usually a set of instructions that nobody could ever live up to. People were always under condemnation. They were continually feeling like they never measured up or that they were not good enough, not righteous enough, or not holy enough. This is when Jesus comes along and says, take My set of instructions. Take My yoke. Learn from Me. Jesus arrives in the midst of our storms of life and says, "Hey, throw some of that stuff overboard because you are living under condemnation."

Are you living under some legalistic idea or some expectation that somebody cast on you? Do you feel as though you don't measure up? Maybe you felt as if you were not good enough for your dad or mom, teacher, or spouse?

> Simplify your life and discover things about the Lord and about yourself that will help you survive.

In effect, Jesus says, "Listen, cast that stuff overboard and take My yoke upon you because you can't live up to what others expect of you." Can you find freedom in that idea? Jesus is saying that if you cast all of this other stuff off of you and obey His instructions, then you will find rest for your soul. There will be a place of safety for you where you can breathe and survive.

4. Focus on the Savior, not the storm.

After the men had gone a long time without food, Paul stood up before them and said: "Men, you should have taken my advice not to sail from Crete; then you would have spared yourselves this damage and loss" (Acts 27:21).

Paul just could not resist saying, "I told you so. If you would have listened to me, you wouldn't be in this mess." Paul goes on to say:

But now I urge you to keep up your courage, because not one of you will be lost; only the ship will be destroyed. Last night an angel of the God whose I am and whom I serve stood beside me and said, "Do not be afraid, Paul. You must stand trial before Caesar; and God has graciously given you the lives of all who sail with you." So keep up your courage, men, for I have faith in God that it will happen just as He told me. Nevertheless, we must run aground on some island (Acts 27:22-26).

When you are in the midst of the storm, you may think that you are going to lose the ship, the cargo, and your very life. That could be, and usually is, the moment when God shows up and speaks hope to you. God has done this many times before. He showed up for Paul and Silas in Acts 16. He showed up minutes before midnight when they felt that all hope was gone, and He brought a breakthrough for them. He was there for Daniel in the middle of the lion's den. He showed up for Peter while he was in prison. Believers were praying for Peter and an angel appeared to him and set him free; he went to the house where the believers were praying. God was there for Moses and the Israelites in Exodus 12. And for the disciples in Matthew 14:

> *During the fourth watch of the night Jesus went out to them, walking on the lake. When the disciples saw Him walking on the lake, they were terrified. "It's a ghost," they said, and cried out in fear. But Jesus immediately said to them: "Take courage! It is I. Don't be afraid"* (Matthew 14:25-27).

The danger for us, if we focus too much on the storm, we will miss the Savior. The plan of the enemy is to cause you to focus so much on your circumstances that you take your eyes off the Author and Finisher of your faith. You become so engrossed in the things that are going on around you that, when that moment comes, you miss Him.

Have you ever been in a place where the Lord has calmed the storms of your life? We know that He can do that. He showed up for the disciples in the center of the lake in the middle of the night, standing there addressing the wind and the waves with the voice of authority to be still. When facing financial disaster, the Lord can bring a breakthrough in a moment, and the storm is calm. You may receive a bad report from the doctor and you are praying, crying, and calling out to the Lord, saying that you need a miracle. You go back and get a good report, everything is good, and the storm is calm.

We know that happens. The problem for us is that He does not always calm the storm. He did not calm the storm for Paul. Sometimes He calms *us* in the midst of the storm. Like the time I had a head-on collision when I was 17. While traveling on Highway 19 in Georgia on a Tuesday afternoon in August, a light rain began to fall. My 1971 Dodge Duster cruised along at 55 mph when suddenly, the rear tires lost contact

> Instead of God standing in the bow of your boat and calming the wind and waves, He may stand over the balcony of your heart and speak peace to your soul.

with the asphalt and the car began to hydroplane. My attempts to regain control were futile, and the impact with the oncoming car was deafening. When my car stopped spinning, I realized that the blood dripping onto my girlfriend was coming from my head. The storm was intense, but in that moment, I experienced a peace that was supernatural!

What can be extremely troubling is that when God calms a storm, we expect Him to do the same thing the next time we find ourselves in the midst of a storm. When He does not do it in our timing, it throws us off. Then we think that God has let us down or disappointed us. But it may be that instead of God standing in the bow of your boat and speaking to the wind and the waves, He stands over the balcony of your heart and speaks peace to your soul. You may just miss Him if you allow yourself to become so focused on the storm that you lose sight of the Savior.

5. Be full of faith and courage.

Acts 27:25-26 says: *"So keep up your courage, men, for I have faith in God that it will happen just as He told me. Nevertheless, we must run aground on some island."*

That Scripture bothers me. We are putting our faith in You, God. We are trusting You and we are believing in a breakthrough. Instead, we end up shipwrecked! Paul stands up and says, "I have faith in God, so take courage. God is going to save us, but we are still going to run aground. The ship is still going to be smashed to pieces." That reality messes with my thinking a little bit. We put our faith in the Lord. We trust Him, yet we're shipwrecked.

For example, you may believe that God is going to heal your dad of cancer, but he dies. Or you believe that God is going to restore your marriage, but your spouse files the divorce papers and marries someone else. What do you do with that? What do you do when you put your faith in the Lord and your ship still runs aground? Does it mean that God is not good? Does it mean He is not trustworthy? Does it change anything about His character or His nature? No!

We cannot understand everything that happens in life, but I do know that God is good. And I know that even if I lose everything, Paul says in Romans 8 that *nothing will separate me from His love.* Nothing! Even if I lose everything I have, I know that I will survive the storm and still have my relationship with Him. Take courage and be full of faith. Having faith does not mean that you get to dictate the outcome; it just means that you trust Him regardless of the outcome.

Mark Twain says this about fear: "Courage is resistance to fear, mastery of fear—not absence of fear." We know that courage is not the absence of fear, but it takes faith to move ahead in spite of the fear. Courage is mentioned 35 times in the Bible and, most of the time, it is used in the form of a command to believers. Examples are "take courage" or "be full of courage."

> **Be strong and very courageous.** *Be careful to obey all the law my servant Moses gave you; do not turn from it to the right or to the left, that you may be successful wherever you go. Do not let this Book of the Law depart from your mouth; meditate on it day and night, so that you may be careful to do everything written in it. Then you will be prosperous and successful. Have I not commanded you?* **Be strong and courageous.** *Do not be terrified; do not be discouraged, for the Lord your God will be with you wherever you go* (Joshua 1:7-9).

Courage is an emotion based on a decision that we make, which activates our faith in God while in the midst of circumstances that can produce fear—the very enemy of faith. Courage is a decision that we make. We make that decision to put our faith in the Lord. It is a decision based on the declaration of the Lord.

In Matthew 14, Christ told the disciples to take courage and to choose courage. The next thing He said was, *"It is I. Don't be afraid."* In other words, Jesus was saying to them, "You can choose courage because I am more than enough. You can choose courage because I am sufficient for you. You can choose courage because I'm going to see you through this. You can choose courage and not be afraid because I am here." And He says the same thing to you and me today. Choose courage. Take courage. If you are in the midst of some storm and it looks like your ship is going to run aground, choose courage. Why? Because He is more than enough.

6. Do not jump ship.

On the fourteenth night we were still being driven across the Adriatic Sea, when about midnight the sailors sensed they were approaching land. They took soundings and found that the water was a hundred and twenty feet deep. A short time later they took soundings again and found it was ninety feet deep. Fearing that we would be dashed against the rocks, they dropped four anchors from the stern and prayed for daylight. In an attempt to escape from the ship, the sailors let the lifeboat down into the sea, pretending they were going to lower some anchors from the bow. Then Paul said to the centurion and the soldiers, "Unless these men stay with the ship, you cannot be saved." So the soldiers cut the ropes that held the lifeboat and let it fall away (Acts 27:27-32).

If you are in the middle of a storm, stick with the plan. Do not jump ship. What has God spoken to you? The tendency for us when we get into the midst of the storm is to come up with a Plan B. That was exactly what these sailors had done. They had come up with a sneaky Plan B so they could creep off the ship and keep from dying. Paul caught them and told them that if they follow through with their plan, it meant not only their death, but also the death of everyone aboard the ship.

What has God said to you? Cut away your Plan B and let God be your Plan A, Plan B, Plan C, Plan Y, and Z. Let Him be every plan you have rather than creating a safety net or back-up plan just in case you think God won't come through. Stand on your faith. Stick with His plan.

7. Do not neglect your basic physical needs.

Just before dawn Paul urged them all to eat. "For the last fourteen days," he said, "you have been in constant suspense and have gone without food—you haven't eaten anything. Now I urge you to take some food. You need it to survive. Not one of you will lose a single hair from his head." After he said this, he took some bread and gave thanks to God in front of them all. Then he broke it and began to eat. They were all encouraged and ate some food themselves (Acts 27:33-36).

In the middle of a storm, it is important to not neglect your basic physical needs. Be wise. Sleep when you can sleep. Proverbs 3 talks about how the Lord can cause your sleep to be sweet even in the midst of disaster. When you become physically tired, you become emotionally and spiritually tired. You may think that a survival technique is to eat a whole quart of ice cream. I am with you on that, but you have got to be wise about what you eat. Eating a steady diet of junk food while in the midst of the storm can deplete your energy. Unhealthy eating can result in sugar rushes that bring highs and lows, which make good decisions difficult. Also, you need to maintain some sort of physical exercise in the midst of the storm because it reduces stress. Equally important is to find some ways to laugh. Proverbs says that laughter is like a medicine. So in the middle of the storm, do not neglect these basic, but very necessary, physical needs.

God gives you survival techniques from the Word of God. He included such detail in Acts 27 so that you would pay attention to these seven things and know how to survive the storms of life. You are going to be there. You may be there now. You are either coming out of a storm, are in the midst of a storm, or you are about to go into another one. Wherever you are in the journey of life, know that you will survive by simplifying, according to the instructions of God's Word.

ENDNOTES

1. "The Old Man and the Gulls" from Paul Harvey's The Rest of the Story by Paul Aurandt, 1977, quoted in Knofel Stanton, Heaven Bound Living (Cincinnati: Standard Publishing, 1989), pp. 79-80.

2. New Testament Greek Lexicon, based on Thayer's and Smith's Bible Dictionary, public domain.

3. John MacArthur, *Matthew 19-23* (Chicago: Moody Press, 1988), 337-338.

Chapter 7

Make Your Life Count—
A Journey of Preservation

Life is short and we have never too much time for
gladdening the hearts of those who are traveling the dark
journey with us. Oh be swift to love, make haste to be kind.
—Henri Fredric Amiel

ONE particular biblical version of the journey of preservation is filled with romance, danger, deception, murder plots, and extravagance along the way to saving an entire nation of people. This journey focuses on a woman who went from a position of relative obscurity to a position of royalty in the king's palace.

MODERN-DAY JOURNEYS OF PRESERVATION

There are many modern-day examples of people who committed their lives to helping preserve the lives of others. Here are just a few.

OSKAR SCHINDLER

The movie *Schindler's List* recalls the life of Oskar Schindler, who risked everything to save as many people as he could from the Nazis during World War II. Schindler was a member of the Nazi party and was a very greedy, stingy German businessman. When the Jews were being deported to Germany from Poland, Schindler saw an opportunity to capitalize on cheap labor. He was building a factory and had bribed some members of the Third Reich to let him have some of the Polish Jews instead of sending them to the concentration camps. Schindler saw the Jews as the labor he needed to produce mess kits for the military. One day, he was in the surrounding hills of the Krakow ghetto where the Jews were housed, and he witnessed the slaughter of many of them. It was so deeply disturbing to Schindler that he began making plans to devise ways to keep the Jews from being sent to the concentration camps. His mission was no longer about maintaining productivity; it was now about preserving lives. He had amassed great wealth and began using more of it to bribe the Nazis so that he could spare the lives of Jews on their way to death in the concentration camps. Historians note that Schindler was responsible for the preservation of some 1,100 Jews.[1]

CORRIE TEN BOOM

Corrie Ten Boom was born into a Christian family in the Netherlands. In 1940, the Nazis began invading the country, making many of the Jewish faith afraid of being captured and sent to death camps. In May 1942, there came a knock at the door of the Ten Boom family and a woman in a nice dress with a suitcase was standing at the door. She feared for her life because her husband had been arrested months earlier. She asked the Ten Boom family if she could stay with them. Over the years, the Ten Boom's home harbored many Jewish people, protecting them from the Nazis. In February 1944, the Ten Boom family was arrested and sent to prison. Ten days later, the father died in prison. In September 1944, Corrie's sister died in prison. On December 25, 1944, Corrie was released from prison due to what she found out later was a clerical error. Within that week, all of the women who were of her same age were killed in the prison where she had been housed. Corrie Ten Boom and her family were willing to lay down their lives for the preservation of other people.[2]

PAUL RUSESABAGINA

Paul Rusesabagina was the manager of Hotel Rwanda, a prominent hotel in Rwanda. In 1994, Rwanda was in chaos. The country was in the midst of civil war. An extremist group was responsible for the genocide of over 800,000 members of the Tutsi tribe. Rusesabagina began to bring members of that tribe into the hotel, harboring them there in an attempt to preserve as many as he could. It has been reported that he was responsible for preserving some 1,200 Rwandans because he was willing to risk his life for the sake of saving others.[3]

Esther: From Obscurity to Royalty

Esther 4 tells the story of a woman who goes from obscurity to a member of royalty residing within the palace. She has been dealt terrible news from her relative, Mordecai, and has a very difficult decision to make. The Bible delivers the heart of the action:

> *When Esther's words were reported to Mordecai, he sent back this answer: "Do not think that because you are in the king's house you alone of all the Jews will escape. For if you remain silent at this time, relief and deliverance for the Jews will arise from another place, but you and your father's family will perish. And who knows but that you have come to royal position for such a time as this?" Then Esther sent this reply to Mordecai: "Go, gather together all the Jews who are in Susa, and fast for me. Do not eat or drink for three days, night or day. I and my maids will fast as you do. When this is done, I will go to the king, even though it is against the law. And if I perish, I perish"* (Esther 4:12-16).

With this drama in the back of your mind, let's return to how Esther reached this point.

The first chapter of Esther introduces King Xerxes, the king of the entire Persian Empire. King Xerxes is a very powerful and wealthy man who declared a festival that lasts 180 days—six months—just to display his wealth and splendor to those in his kingdom. At the end of the 180 days, he has a banquet that lasts seven days. This was an open invitation to everyone to enjoy unlimited food and wine. Simultaneously, Queen Vashti decides that she is going to have a banquet for some of the women in the land. In the midst of the feast, King Xerxes decides that he wants to show Queen Vashti off to his people because she is so beautiful. Queen Vashti could be likened to a "trophy wife" in today's society. He summons her to his banquet, but she refuses because she does not want to be paraded in front of everyone.

It is easy to see how her refusal would infuriate King Xerxes. He seeks the counsel of those around him about how to respond to Queen Vashti. They recommend that he forbid her to come into his presence again and dethrone her as queen. He agrees. The second chapter opens with King Xerxes searching for a new queen and wife. There is an extensive process to gather all of the beautiful young virgins in the Persian Empire and bring them to the palace.

A young, beautiful Jewish girl by the name of Esther is invited to the palace. This stay at the palace is not for a day or a week, but for 12 months to receive the best treatment to prepare her to meet the king.

The Bible says that Esther finds great favor with the man who is in charge of all these young virgins, and he gives her special treatment. When it is time for King Xerxes' elaborate beauty pageant, all of the young virgins are paraded in front of him so he can pick his new wife and queen. Xerxes selects Esther. At the end of the second chapter, something very important happens that sets up this journey of preservation. It should be noted that Esther is an orphan being raised by her older relative, Mordecai, who took her into his household and became her guardian.

During the 12 months when Esther is in the palace and after being selected as queen, Mordecai is very interested in what is going on; he sits outside of the king's gates every day so that he can keep tabs on Esther. One day, he overhears a conversation between two of the king's officers who are angry with the king. These two men decide to kill King Xerxes. When Mordecai overhears the plot, he sends word to Esther. She goes to the king and tells him about the plot. They verify the story and the two men are hanged. The Bible says that Mordecai's name is then recorded in the official documents of the palace as the man who spared King Xerxes' life.

THE DRAMA OF PRESERVATION

The plot thickens in chapter 3. Haman, a very prominent man in the king's palace, is promoted to the position of prime minister of the Persian Empire. Haman is an arrogant man full of pride. He expects people to bow down to him when walking through the streets. All the people in the empire do this except Mordecai. He is a God-fearing Jew who refuses to bow his knee to anyone except Yahweh. Haman becomes so furious that he deceives King Xerxes into issuing an edict that would annihilate all of the Jews in the land. The official signet ring of King Xerxes stamps the edict, and it goes throughout the entire land.

In the beginning of the fourth chapter of Esther, the Jews, along with Mordecai, are in great distress. Someone who passes by Mordecai, who is seated in front of the King's gate, sees that he is dressed in sack cloths and has ashes on his feet. They report this to Queen Esther. She does not know about the edict, so she sends one of the king's attendants to find out what is going on with Mordecai. She has them take some clothes to him and help him clean himself up. The attendant asks Mordecai why he is so distressed. Mordecai responds by showing the attendant the edict and explains that it says that all of the Jews, including him, are to be killed. He asks the attendant to plead with Esther to talk to the king so that something might be done to save them. The action picks up in Esther 4:

Hathach went back and reported to Esther what Mordecai had said. Then she instructed him to say to Mordecai, "All the king's officials and the people of the royal provinces know that for any man or woman who approaches the king in the inner court without being summoned the king has but one law: that he be put to death. The only exception to this is for the king to extend the gold scepter to him and spare his life. But thirty days have passed since I was called to go to the king" (Esther 4:9-11).

Esther sends a message back to Mordecai telling him that it is not as easy as he thinks because she cannot go talk to the king whenever she wants. Esther knows that unless the king calls for her, she cannot go to him without risking death or hoping that he lowers his golden scepter to avoid a death sentence.

> *When Esther's words were reported to Mordecai, he sent back this answer: "Do not think that because you are in the king's house you alone of all the Jews will escape. For if you remain silent at this time, relief and deliverance for the Jews will arise from another place, but you and your father's family will perish. And who knows but that you have come to royal position for such a time as this?"* (Esther 4:12-14)

Mordecai's response is to get Esther to think that, perhaps, there was a reason why she was selected as queen in terms of having someone in the right place to enable the preservation of the Jewish people. It is clear that Esther dwells on this idea when she provides this order to Mordecai:

> *Then Esther sent this reply to Mordecai: "Go, gather together all the Jews who are in Susa, and fast for me. Do not eat or drink for three days, night or day. I and my maids will fast as you do. When this is done, I will go to the king, even though it is against the law. And if I perish, I perish"* (Esther 4:15-16).

YOUR JOURNEY OF PRESERVATION INVOLVES PRESERVING OTHERS

Before revealing the amazing ending to this dramatic story, it is important to take a moment to think about your own journey of preservation. Many of the events that happen in this story have application for you today.

First, you must remember that your life has purpose and a God-designed destiny. You exist for more than just taking up space on this planet. You are here for more than just breathing in air and giving off carbon dioxide. Your purpose involves more than playing video games, climbing the corporate ladder, becoming a sports star, making money, or hooking up with someone other than your spouse. Instead, your purpose and your destiny involve the preservation of others. Often, it is difficult to live according to your purpose because society teaches that it is more important to be concerned about the preservation of self rather than the preservation of others.

To help you focus on your true purpose, there are three things to note about the preservation of others:

1. We are *called* to preserve the lives of others.

You are the salt of the earth. But if the salt loses its saltiness, how can it be made salty again? It is no longer good for anything, except to be thrown out and trampled by men (Matthew 5:13).

Although Jesus is talking to the disciples, He is also talking to you. Jesus is saying that you are the salt of the earth, and if you lose your saltiness, then how can you be made salty again? Salt that isn't salty is no good anymore and should be thrown out and trampled. You need to add flavor to the lives of others and become a preserving agent in people's lives.

The only way you can stop others from spiritual decay is to get involved in their lives. The problem with getting involved in the lives of others is that it can become messy and inconvenient. Involvement can also require giving things that you may not be willing to give—time, love, financial support.

You can slide the salt shaker across the table from alongside your bowl of green beans, grits, or French fries and leave it there for hours. However, this will not change the flavor of the food unless you turn it over and pour some of it from the salt shaker. You may want to get near people, but you may put up so many walls to protect yourself from really getting involved in their lives, that you're not helping them or yourself. God calls us to get involved by leaving our place of comfort, adding flavor, and serving as the preserving agent in the lives of other people.

Salt is made up of two elements: sodium and chloride. Sodium is always found in combination with other elements. Chloride, by itself, is very deadly. However, when it is combined with sodium, chloride becomes something very useful—something most people use every day. Truth and love are like sodium and chloride. Love by itself can be flighty; it can be blind; and it is willing to combine itself with any doctrine or thought that comes along. Likewise, truth by itself can be deadly and offensive.

You may have a lot of love but no truth. This can do just as much damage as someone who has truth but no love. Jesus was describing truth and love coming together in our lives so that it would turn us into the salt of the earth. In this way, we combine love and truth in order to add flavor and preservation to the lives of others.

2. We are *capable* of preserving the lives of others.

It is common for God to call us to things that are, in our estimation, beyond our natural ability. However, it is the Lord who makes us capable. Esther was given the calling to preserve the lives of others, and Mordecai sends the word to her as the voice of the Lord puts this journey of preservation into action.

> You need to add flavor to the lives of others and become a preserving agent in their lives.
>
>

Esther's confidence is tied up in her external beauty. She knows that her beauty is desired and serves as external offerings. It is important to remember that capability has little to do with our talents. Rather, it has everything to do with the One who calls us. For us to find that capability and bring it out means that we have to be people of obedience. Even Mary, the mother of Jesus, understands this as He is thrust into the ministry and performs His first miracle at a wedding. When Mary calls on Him to bring forth wine, Jesus tells her that it is before His time. Instead of debating with Him, Mary turns to the disciples and says, "Whatever He tells you to do, do it." The mother of Jesus realizes that our capability is limited only by the degree to which we are willing to obey.

Obedience is the highest form of worship. The atmosphere of obedience is the atmosphere in which God visits, so our capability is—or should be—wrapped up in Him. In fact, confidence in our ability is the greatest detriment to Him thrusting us into our destiny. Throughout the Scriptures, we see an interesting principle concerning our trust in Him. Whatever it was that God called people into—whether it was armies opposing one another or man-to-man combat—those on the Lord's side were always smaller in number or smaller in stature. The Lord wants us to be completely dependent upon Him.

Our obedience has to be driven by our realization of who He says He is. The greatest display from the Lord comes from the people who are obedient. When He calls us, He also makes us capable of preserving the lives of others. Our capability to do so is driven by the degree to which we are willing to obey. In Exodus 4, the Lord calls Moses to do something that was beyond his natural ability. The Lord appears to him in a burning bush, calls him into ministry, and tells Moses what he is to do. Moses answers in Exodus 4:

Moses answered, "What if they do not believe me or listen to me and say, 'The Lord did not appear to you?'" Then the Lord said to him, "What is that in your hand?" "A staff," he replied (Exodus 4:1-2).

Think about this for a moment. There is a bush that is burning and not being consumed. The voice of God is coming from it, and Moses says, "What if they do not believe that You are the One who sent me?" You are probably wondering: *Why doesn't the bush burn up Moses for not believing?* Sometimes we are more interested in how we are perceived by people than by the calling of the Lord. The Lord gives a great response, in essence saying: "Moses, what is in your hand? Sure it's just a stick but one that you purchased through suffering in the wilderness. If you give Me that, I will perform miraculous signs with it. Just obey Me."

We also gain our capability from the Lord—the One who is sending us, the One who is going with us, and the One who is in us. Perspective is everything. It is not about our resources or our level of gifting or talent. Our capability is in the One who goes with us and the One who is in us. As previously mentioned, the Lord's side is always outnumbered in the natural. In fact, every story in Scripture makes this point. For example, Gideon has an army of 32,000. They did not have a prayer when it came time to battling the opposing army of 192,000 (see Judges 7).[4] Gideon is told to reduce his army to 10,000 and, even after that, the Lord tells Gideon that he still has too many men. It is almost comical.

The Lord asks: "Do you want to give your external offering where you feel like it makes sense, and do you believe that you have what it takes?" Or, are you going to base your confidence on a revelation of who He is?

Our capacity to even love Him is birthed out of a revelation of His love for us. John said, *"We love because He first loved us"* (1 John 4:19). That means that we only have the ability to love when we have a revelation of Him, so our capability is based on our obedience and also on our revelation. The Bible says, *"Be strong and courageous. Do not be afraid or terrified because of them, for the Lord your God goes with you; He will never leave you nor forsake you"* (Deut. 31:6). He not only goes with us; He is also in us. We need to become a people who realize that God lives inside us, because that is where our authority emanates.

3. We are *commanded* to preserve the lives of others.

In Colossians 1:27, it says, *"To them God has chosen to make known among the Gentiles the glorious riches of this mystery, which is Christ in you, the hope of glory."* We are capable of preserving the lives of other people when we see and feel the One who is sending us in our obedience, the One who is going with us, and the One who is in us. Not only are we called, but also the implication of calling is that we have the option to say yes or no to Him who is calling us. However, He not only gives us a revelation of the fact that we are capable, but He also commands us to preserve the lives of other people. There is no way out of this assignment.

The Bible says, *"My command is this: Love each other as I have loved you. Greater love has no one than this, that he lay down his life for his friends"* (John 15:12-13). The command is that we lay down our lives for others. Esther counted the cost and she said, "If I perish, I perish." We have to become a people with a united voice that cries out from the Book of Hebrews: "We are not of those who shrink back and are destroyed. But we are of those who believe and who are saved."

COUNTING THE COST

When Esther counts the cost, she says to tell Mordecai that if she is not received by the king, then she will die. She understands now that she had been called to her current position. She knows it is not just about a person's external offerings. As you think about these ideas, consider these Scriptures:

That is why I am suffering as I am. Yet I am not ashamed, because I know whom I have believed, and am convinced that He is able to guard what I have entrusted to Him for that day (2 Timothy 1:12).

But we have this treasure in jars of clay to show that this all-surpassing power is from God and not from us (2 Corinthians 4:7).

You, dear children, are from God and have overcome them, because the One who is in you is greater than the one who is in the world. They are from the world and therefore speak from the viewpoint of the world, and the world listens to them (1 John 4:4-5).

Through our weaknesses, cracks, struggles, and lack of capabilities, the Lord is seen. It is the upside-down kingdom. It is the one who is low who has been made high. It is the one who recognizes their weakness. It is the one who displays the greatest picture and reality of his or her strength. We are capable because we obey Him. We are capable because He goes with us. And we are capable because He is in us.

Paul said in Philippians 4 that *"I can do anything through Christ."* How many times are we discouraged because we allow this restricted reality to drive us? We need to focus on the fact that we can do anything through Christ. In Colossians 1, the mystery that has been kept hidden for ages is that Christ is in you so that there is the hope of glory.

THE END OF ESTHER'S DRAMATIC JOURNEY OF PRESERVATION

Let's return to Esther's dramatic decision and how she decides where her journey of preservation will take her. Esther approaches King Xerxes, but she does not know if she will die or not. The King places his scepter over her and spares her. He asks Esther about her request and promises that he will do anything for her up to half his kingdom. At this point she illustrates the old adage that the best way to a man's heart is through his stomach. Esther invites King Xerxes and Haman to a meal that she has prepared for them. They come and sit down at a wonderful great meal that she has prepared. The suspense about her request is unsettling for King Xerxes. Esther finally says that her request is for the king and Haman to join her at a banquet the following night.

The Bible says that King Xerxes cannot sleep that night, so he gets up in the middle of the night. He pulls out the palace's official documents and starts reading through what has been recorded throughout his rule. He stumbles across the story of a man by the name of Mordecai who had spared his life by uncovering a plot. King Xerxes wonders if anything was ever done for this man. He asks his attendants and they tell him that nothing was ever done, so he decides to honor Mordecai the very next day.

In the meantime, Haman is proud that he is the only one invited to the banquet. On his way home to tell his wife, he passes Mordecai who again does not bow down to him. Haman goes home and tells his wife and his friends about the invitation to a fine dinner with Queen Esther. He also relates to his wife about how furious he is with Mordecai. His wife suggests that he build gallows and ask the king to have Mordecai put to death on them tomorrow. Immediately, Haman orders workers to build the gallows that night.

> The Lord always has a way of turning the tables on the enemy.
>
>

The next morning, the king asks Haman what should be done for a man the king wishes to honor. Haman automatically assumes that the king is talking about him. He is so prideful that he comes up with a grandiose idea—such a man should be placed on one of the royal stallions of the palace, dressed in a royal robe, and paraded through the city streets with someone who walks alongside and says, "This is what is done for the man that the king wishes to honor." All the while, Haman is picturing himself on the horse.

King Xerxes tells him what a wonderful idea that is and then tells him to go and do that for Mordecai—the man Haman despises, the one he had planned to murder. Now he has to go dress Mordecai in a fine robe and walk him through the city streets.

That night they go to the banquet to eat and drink again. The King cannot stand it anymore, and again implores Esther to tell him her request so that he can give her up to half his kingdom. She pulls out a copy of the edict and tells him that the man who deceived him into writing this will destroy her and her people. She then says to King Xerxes that she wants this man dead. He looks at it, sees his seal, and asks who would do this and deceive him like this. Esther points to the man across the table and says, "This evil man, Haman."

King Xerxes is so furious that he has to walk out of the room to calm down. Haman realizes that his fate rests in the hands of Queen Esther. He throws himself at her feet and begins begging for his life. King Xerxes walks back into the room and sees Haman grabbing the queen and thinks that he is trying to rape his wife. He immediately orders that Haman be killed and learns that gallows had been built the day before. He orders that Haman be hung on his own gallows.

The Lord always has a way of turning the tables on the enemy. The Bible says, *"And having disarmed the powers and authorities, He made a public spectacle of them, triumphing over them by the cross"* (Col. 2:15). The enemy wants you to be consumed with self-preservation rather than the preservation of others. If you step out and obey the Lord, then the Lord will turn the tables on the enemy so that the very things that the enemy was trying to use to destroy you will be the very things used to expose him.

EMULATE ESTHER

I want to pause here and talk about a critical issue that women face in today's society that causes women to compare themselves to others. This mentality originates from a carnal nature and is not the nature of the Lord. It is important that every woman receive freedom from the Lord so that they do not compare their destiny, their calling, or their purpose in life to that of other women. What God has called other women to do is different from what God has called you to do.

Do not compare yourself with what other women do for the Lord, how they worship, raise their kids, or what they do in the Body of Christ. Instead, respond to His voice and what He says to *you*. He created you uniquely for who He wants you to be. You cannot function in someone else's calling or someone else's destiny. You must function within God's plan for you, your calling—learn to be secure in who He has called you to be.

LIVING TO PRESERVE OTHERS

A quote at the Alamo on the trail of facts from one of the captains of the armies says: "We would rather die in these trenches than give them over to the enemy."

The Lord is looking for people who will say, "I will give my life for this thing so that the lives of others may be preserved." Perhaps you know people who the enemy has tried to discourage or depress. When will we stand with one another and say, "I will die with you fighting this thing rather than give ground over to the enemy"? When will we say, "No, we will die in these trenches, and if I perish, I perish, but on my watch, this ground will not be willfully given over to the enemy"? We have been called to lay down our lives. The Bible says:

I eagerly expect and hope that I will in no way be ashamed, but will have sufficient courage so that now as always

Christ will be exalted in my body, whether by life or by death. For to me, to live is Christ and to die is gain (Philippians 1:20-21).

There are young people within the church and their mantra is: "By life or by death, I am going to follow You. I am going to lay down my life as an intercessor between heaven and earth that Your people may get the message that it is not about our own insecurities or rejections." Most of the time, it is not about a physical death. Living in death can be more difficult than just giving your life over as a hero. As such, we are called to live as dead to our own desires because He has commanded us to lay down our lives. Consider these Scriptures:

But you will receive power when the Holy Spirit comes on you; and you will be My witnesses in Jerusalem, and in all Judea and Samaria, and to the ends of the earth (Acts 1:8).

The word *witness* translates as martyr. Those who lay down their lives for the cause of the gospel are martyrs. As Esther said, "If I perish, I perish."

The Spirit and the bride say, "Come!" And let him who hears say, "Come!" Whoever is thirsty, let him come; and whoever wishes, let him take the free gift of the water of life (Revelation 22:17).

> Choosing to do anything outside of what God has called you to do results in a miserable life.

The cry of Heaven is that somehow our voices will join the serenade of the spirit, beckoning the lost ones—those who are perishing—to Himself that the voice of the bride will join the voice of the spirit and say, "Come," so that the lives of others might be preserved.

> Esther decided that it would be better to die trying to preserve the lives of her people than to die thinking only of herself.

"Even now," declares the Lord, "return to Me with all your heart, with fasting and weeping and mourning. Rend your heart and not your garments. Return to the Lord your God, for He is gracious and compassionate, slow to anger and abounding in love, and He relents from sending calamity" (Joel 2:12-13).

The garments in this last Scripture passage represent the calling of the priests. In that day and culture, when people would mourn a death or a difficult situation, they would tear their clothes as a sign of grieving. However, there was a law with the penalty of death that stated that the priests were never to tear their clothes. In other words, for us, no matter what the circumstances or the difficulties of life are, you can never tear away your calling as the intercessor of the most high God. And when the prophet says that he is speaking of the last days of revival that we are all calling out for but your heart does not match the call, do not tear the call; instead, tear your heart. We have all been given the authority and ability from the One who is within us.

This is a real challenge because, in the world, we are taught to preserve our own lives. However, the Kingdom of God is about preserving the lives of others. You have been called to do that. You are capable of doing that. You are commanded to do that. This is because you are made for this; you are created for this; and you are built for this. Choosing to do anything outside of what God has called you to do will result in a miserable life.

The need to preserve others has been put inside of us—we all have a little bit of Indiana Jones in us, a desire for thrill and adventure. God put that in us because He did not want us to dumb down our faith and live a boring life. Instead, He wants us to be involved in the lives of other people. The Bible says, *"For we are God's workmanship, created in Christ Jesus to do good works, which God prepared in advance for us to do"* (Eph. 2:10).

Many people are miserable because they are living outside of their purpose and destiny. As a result, they are making those around them miserable. They become irritable and judgmental because they are doing something that God never called them to do or they are trying to live outside of their existence. They become restless and end up dying a slow spiritual death.

Esther decided that it would be better to die trying to preserve the lives of the Jewish people than to die thinking only of herself. Esther believed that it was better to die trying to do God's will than to live in apathy and disobedience. You never know what it is to truly live until you reach the place in your journey where you are truly willing to die.

ENDNOTES

1. http://en.wikipedia.org/wiki/Oskar_Schindler.

2. http://en.wikipedia.org/wiki/Corrie_Ten_Boom.

3. http://en.wikipedia.org/wiki/Paul_Rusesabagina.

4. Robert Jamieson, A. R. Fausset, and David Brown, *Commentary Critical and Explanatory on the Whole Bible*, published in 1871.

Chapter 8

Who Could Have Imagined?— A Journey of Transformation

He who is outside his door already has
a hard part of his journey behind him.
—Dutch Proverb

THE television is full of shows about transformation. For instance, on HGTV they completely transform a closet, garage, yard, or old bathroom within the 30- or 60-minute show. The reason these programs are popular is because everyone has a closet, garage, yard, or bathroom in need of a major transformation, and all of us like positive change.

YOUR TRANSFORMATION TIMELINE

The word *transformation* means a thorough or dramatic change in appearance or form. Transformation is both instantaneous and progressive. Transformation can happen in a moment, but it can also take a lifetime. Alan Redpath, a former pastor of the historic Moody Bible Church in Chicago, Illinois, said, "The conversion of a soul is the miracle of a moment. The manufacturer of a saint is the task of a lifetime."[1]

We have been conditioned to accept unreasonable timelines like those presented on television. We all want to experience instant gratification where transformation is immediate. However, the transformation of a life is completely different from the transformation of a closet or a garage. Transforming to the image of God is a life-long project requiring patience, commitment, hard work, and diligence. After all, the transformation of a life is the most powerful transformation known.

If and when God makes a transformation in our lives, it does not happen in the span of 30 minutes or an hour. Lacking a sense of reality, we grow impatient with His version of the transformation process. Yet, despite our impatience, God still invites us to take this journey of transformation with Him.

Have you ever thought about an area of your life that needs transformation? One of the greatest Scriptures about transformation is found in First Peter:

> *See, I lay a stone in Zion, a chosen and precious cornerstone, and the one who trusts in Him will never be put to shame. Now to you who believe, this stone is precious. But to those who do not believe, the stone the builders rejected has become the capstone, and, a stone that causes men to stumble and a rock that makes them fall. They stumble because they disobey the message—which is also what they were destined for. But you are a chosen people, a royal priesthood, a holy nation, a people belonging to God, that you may declare the praises of Him who called you out of darkness into His wonderful light. Once you were not a people, but now you are the people of God; once you had not received mercy, but now you have received mercy* (1 Peter 2:6-10).

In this passage, the stone is Jesus, who provides the power for transformation. Ask yourself, have you been called out of the darkness and declared righteous in His wonderful light? You serve a God who has the power and the ability to transform—to take that nasty, cluttered closet that represents an area of your life and completely transform it.

ON GOD'S RADAR SCREEN

Acts 9 contains one of the most illustrative life transformations recorded in Scripture. It is the story of Saul found in Acts 9:1-2, which paints this picture:

> *Meanwhile, Saul was still breathing out murderous threats against the Lord's disciples. He went to the high priest and asked him for letters to the synagogues in Damascus, so that if he found any there who belonged to the Way, whether men or women, he might take them as prisoners to Jerusalem (Acts 9:1-2).*

The first glimpse of Saul is not a pretty one. In Acts 6, there is a devout man named Stephen. He has been called before the Sanhedrin because they are upset with the things he is saying. Some people have been bribed to falsely accuse Stephen of heresy and stir up the crowd. This works the crowd up to a fevered pitch and they drive Stephen out of the city on the northern side of Jerusalem. Outside of the city wall and gate, they begin pummeling him with stones until he falls down dead. In Acts 7, Saul is described as standing at the scene like a terrorist with the blood of a martyr staining his clothes. The Bible says that he is smiling as he holds the coats of those who are stoning Stephen. Saul is reveling in the moment and seems to enjoy what is happening to this Stephen (Acts 8:1).

Saul turns his attention to Damascus, which is 100 miles away. Although there are other little cities where Saul could go to arrest people for following Christ, Saul wants to score big and knows that Damascus is a haven for those who are trying to escape persecution. Everyone is well-aware of Saul's reputation as a lunatic and blood-thirsty man. Despite

Your plans may be interrupted by God!

his zealous ways, Saul is well-educated and well-versed in the poetry of the Scriptures. However, he believes that the Christians have jeopardized the Jewish tradition and the Jewish faith.

Since he feels threatened by the Christians, Saul's whole plan is to eliminate them as stated in Acts 6 and 7. Saul knows that he can find plenty of people who follow Christ if he goes to Damascus. He hopes that his actions will be rewarded and that he will become a member of the Sanhedrin.

However, his plans are interrupted by God, as he embarks on this journey to Damascus to destroy the followers of Christ:

> *As he neared Damascus on his journey, suddenly a light from heaven flashed around him. He fell to the ground and heard a voice say to him, "Saul, Saul, why do you persecute Me?" "Who are you, Lord?" Saul asked. "I am Jesus, whom you are persecuting," he replied. "Now get up and go into the city, and you will be told what you must do." The men traveling with Saul stood there speechless; they heard the sound but did not see anyone* (Acts 9:3-7).

For the first time, Saul sees himself reduced to a desperate dependant. He is on the ground with his face buried in the dirt. He is blind and hears a voice. He does not recognize the voice or know where it is coming from. Saul has been living in spiritual darkness even though he believes that he is very religious. This spiritual darkness is written about in the Bible:

> *When Jesus spoke again to the people, He said, "I am the light of the world. Whoever follows Me will never walk in darkness, but will have the light of life"* (John 8:12).

Saul has no idea about the light shining around him. Later, when Paul (previously known as Saul) is writing a letter to the Corinthians, it is ironic when he says:

> *For God, who said, "Let light shine out of darkness," made His light shine in our hearts to give us the light of the knowledge of the glory of God in the face of Christ* (2 Corinthians 4:6).

Paul writes from a first-hand account with the Messiah. Paul tells the Corinthian church that he knows from experience what he is talking about. In essence, he is saying, "I was face down in the dirt. There was bright light around me. I didn't know who or what was going on. Let me tell you, the light came into my heart. I was called out of the darkness into the marvelous light of the Lord. I came face to face with Him and, all of a sudden, I had knowledge of the glory of God."

What made this encounter with Jesus so incredible is that Jesus had already been crucified, so Saul did not consider Him a threat or a problem. Saul has no issue with Him; it is with the people who were trying to keep the "Christian" movement going. The other amazing thing about this encounter is the fact that Saul the terrorist and murderer was on God's radar screen. God even called him by name. Isn't that amazing? Just think, no matter how far away you get from God, you are still on His radar screen.

Here is a guy determined to annihilate anyone who is following Christ. Yet God sends His personal message: "I know your name. I know where you are. I know what you are up to and I'm still absolutely crazy about you. And I've got plans for you that go way beyond what you had in mind." Saul responds to the voice and says: "Who are you, Lord?"

> No matter how far away you get from God, you are still on His radar screen.

The Greek word for Lord is *kyrios*. It is a term of respect, like using the word *sir*. Since Saul is face down in the dirt and blind, he figures that this is not the time to be arrogant or cocky. It does not seem like the right time to whip out his credentials and say, "Hey, do you know who you are messing with?" The response that comes back to Saul completely shocks and surprises him: "I'm Jesus whom you are persecuting." Saul is astonished and thinks this must be impossible since he could not possibly be speaking to a dead man. It is easy to imagine all the things running through Saul's mind as well as the deafening silence that follows as he lays face down in the dirt.

SAUL'S MOMENT OF TRANSFORMATION

All of a sudden, Saul's journey—his life, thinking, goals, hopes, and his future—comes to a screeching halt and his direction is reversed. Saul is transformed from a terrorist and a murderer to a believer. Everything changes when he is confronted with the resurrected Jesus. There is irony in the words Paul wrote to the Ephesians 2:8-9, *"For it is by grace you have been saved, through faith—and this not from yourselves, it is the gift of God—not by works, so that no one can boast."* Paul knew that he could not take credit for the divine gift of transformation he experienced.

> *Saul got up from the ground, but when he opened his eyes he could see nothing. So they led him by the hand into Damascus. For three days he was blind, and did not eat or drink anything* (Acts 9:8-9).

Saul's life is completely transformed. A man named Ananias, who was a very well-known and respected follower of Christ in Damascus, receives a vision from God. His task is to go to a house where he will find a man by the name of Saul. Ananias is concerned because he knows all about Saul. Yet God has told him to find Saul and pray for him. Sometimes, it requires great faith to do the things that the Lord wants us to do.

Ananias obeys the Lord by finding Saul and praying for him. The Bible says that something like scales fall from Saul's eyes. Saul becomes a great father of the faith. He writes most of what is known as the New Testament, and people have feasted on these truths for centuries.

The Four Truths of Transformation

Transformation is amazing and powerful, but it can be very scary as well. To alleviate any fear, focus on these four truths about transformation:

1. Godly transformation can be messy.

Usually that closet, garage, or yard needing transformation is at its absolute worst before you take on the project. Often, that mess is what motivates you. Garages, closets, and yards, if left unattended, do not get organized by themselves. They only get worse, more chaotic, and more disorganized.

The same thing is true about our lives. The moment of transformation is usually when we are at our worst and at our greatest need. Even after the transformation process begins, it can continue to be very messy. Think about remodeling your house. You may be tasting sawdust and sheetrock dust in everything you eat. There are paint rollers and tarps everywhere.

Or you decide that you are going to take on the closet, and one thing leads to another, and then another. The project gets worse before it gets better. Sometimes God has to tear out walls in your life and push through the clutter and all of the garbage to decide what stuff needs to go to the dumpster and what should stay. It can be messy when God starts to

> The mess that God makes leads to transformation.
>
>

transform your life. The mess you make tends to lead to more mess, but the mess that God makes leads to transformation.

2. Godly transformation can be sudden.

The fact that a transformation can be sudden is what makes it so complex and beautiful. God is so masterful at breaking into your life, schedule, and plans. He can disrupt what is going on in your life, break into your miserable existence when you are at the bar; dating that guy you should not be dating; or wracked with financial burdens and don't know what to do. God is so masterful at bringing the divine into your life. That is what He did with Saul. The supernatural experience comes out of nowhere and is totally unexpected. God just breaks into his life and totally transforms it. Like a whirlwind when you least expect it, God catches you when you are vulnerable, and He totally changes your life.

3. Godly transformation will sometimes blind us to the temporal and awaken us to the spiritual.

Saul is completely blind in a spiritual sense. However, God blinds him to the natural, or temporal, things in order to awaken him to the eternal. Sometimes God will blind you to the things that are right in front of your face so that you do not know what to do. You cannot make a decision about your job. You do not know what to do about a financial crisis. God does this to awaken you to spiritual sight and eternal truths. That is why Elisha could see the angels that were in the hills around them but his servant could not see them until he prayed (see 2 Kings 6:17). God wants to awaken you and open your eyes spiritually so that you can see beyond the obvious. The old cliché is true. You don't see the forest for the trees. However, God helps you overcome this blindness.

4. Godly transformation will affect every area of your life.

Suddenly, the very people that Saul came to arrest are the people he is now hanging out with. He is one of them. Godly transformation will change your desires, your relationships, your habits, and even your thought processes. Things that you had in your life for years—and even decades—can change because of the transforming power of God. Your journey of transformation leads you from death to life. Saul's life is so transformed that he is no longer referred to as Saul—Paul is transformed through the power and grace of God.

Skunks and Spaniels:
A Story of Transformation

When we bought a house in a subdivision several years ago, God immediately gave Melanie and me a burden for the many families who were unchurched and unbelievers. Two doors down lived Mike and Michelle. Late-night weekend parties were a common occurrence at their house.

At first, we resorted to the usual waves from one yard to the next, or the occasional "hello" at the neighborhood pool. Something about this couple made me want to reach out to them with every bit of soul-winning ability I could muster. However, another part of me, in all honesty, said, "You are wasting your time with them. You will never be able to reach them." Every attempt we made at building relationship or establishing communication seemed to be met with cold replies, at best. I carried on an awkward conversation with Mike about his pressure washer, invited him over for a pick-up basketball game, and sent an invitation with a personal note for our church's Easter production. Nothing! Each time they drove by our house, I prayed, "Father, please open some door and help me to seize some opportunity to talk with Mike and Michelle. Touch their hearts and draw them to you." Three years went by with no apparent changes.

In the meantime, we encountered something in our subdivision that we had never encountered up close and personal—skunks! I opened the front door very early one Sunday morning and let Stormie, our cocker spaniel, out for her morning "business" walk. When I opened the door again, Stormie ran into the house, followed by one of the most horrid smells I have ever known. She had taken a direct hit by a skunk, right in our front yard. The weeks that followed were filled with countless bathings with tomato juice, lemon juice, special skunk deodorizer and dog shampoo, as well as trying to air out the house.

Late one afternoon, while working in the yard, the spirit of God prompted my heart with this thought: "Go now and tell Mike about the skunk." The thought seemed both humorous and absurd. I began to build my argument with God. "God that's ridiculous! What will I say to him about a skunk? He already thinks I'm odd. I just can't do that." But the thought only intensified, and after a ten-minute wrestling match with the Lord, He won out. Off I went, still vacillating between risk and reason, obedience and disobedience, courage and fear with each step that took me nearer their house. "Maybe no one is home," I thought as I approached the front door. But the door opened, and I went into some strange discourse with Mike about skunks being on the loose in the neighborhood, and that he might want to keep a close eye on his dog. Man did I feel foolish! "Thanks," Mike said. "I'm a little out of touch with what is going on. I've been at the hospital for the past seven days with Michelle. She has had some problems with her pregnancy and needed surgery."

Wow! Suddenly there was an opening and the opportunity I had been praying for. We began responding with meals, and Melanie visited regularly to check on Michelle. Over three years of praying began to take shape. Several weeks later, Michelle went into labor and delivered a healthy girl, although she was eight weeks premature. I was able to go to the hospital several times and pray with Mike and Michelle and encourage them with words of faith and hope. The hard outer shell began to peel away as God showed his faithfulness to them in a way that touched them deeply, through their new baby girl.

The day finally arrived when they would be able to take Maggie home from the hospital. We took a gift by their home, and with tears in his eyes Mike thanked us for the numerous ways we had helped them through their crisis. "We're gonna come to your church soon, too," he said on that January afternoon. And weeks later, on Easter Sunday, they did just that. God continued to touch their hearts, they surrendered their lives to Christ, and He transformed them from darkness to light.

GOD HAS SELECTED YOU FOR TRANSFORMATION

Take a moment and revisit your life. Imagine crying every day. Your life is miserable and in shambles. Yet God has you on His radar screen and says, "I've got some great plans for you that go way beyond the misery you are living in and go way beyond the mess that you have made of the closet or garage of your life."

If you think you were living a life of utter despair and woke up one day and decided that you were going to serve Jesus, it did not happen that

God handpicked *you.*

way. He picked you. He chose you. He loved you. When you were at your worst, God kept setting things up for a moment of transformation for you because He is absolutely crazy about you. He loves you so much. You did not choose Him. God handpicked you. As John 15:16 says, *"You did not choose Me, but I chose you and appointed you to go and bear fruit—fruit that will last. Then the Father will give you whatever you ask in My name."*

It is estimated that the population of the planet will reach 7 billion people by 2012. Currently, the population stands at 6.7 billion people. What is truly amazing is that, out of 6.7 billion people, the Lord knows your name. He even knows your middle name that you keep secret from everyone. He has chosen *you.* Let Him transform you.

ENDNOTE

1.   Alan Redpath, *Making of a Man of God: The Lessons from the Life of David* (Grand Rapids, MI: Revell, 2004), back cover.

Chapter 9

Free At Last!—
A Journey of Deliverance

You must remain focused on your journey to greatness.
—Les Brown

A T one time or another, everyone has wanted to escape from a particular moment or situation. It could involve a frustrating job or a bad relationship. It might be the apartment or neighborhood where you live. Whatever that moment or situation may be, it surely made you want to scream, "Get me out of here!"

As kids, my friends and I would get on rides at amusement parks to try and make ourselves sick. No matter how much food we would eat before the rides, we could not do it. However, something happened to my body when I got a little older. That reality sunk in when I was at a fair several years ago.

I had just eaten a big greasy cheeseburger when my friends and I got on a ride that spins you around and around. It did not take much more than about 30 seconds on the ride until my stomach was queasy and that this was just not fun anymore. I turned all colors. Sweat was dripping off of me. The cheeseburger felt like it was going to make a return appearance. I just kept praying that I would not throw up in front of my friends. It seemed the ride was extra long, so I had to hang on and pray that it would end soon. I thanked Jesus when the ride slowed down and stopped. Suddenly, it started up again. This time it was going *backward* at the same lightning and nauseating speed. I wanted out. All I could think was, *Please, God, just deliver me!*

The word *deliverance* simply means the action of being rescued or set free. It might be connected to a story like the one you just read or it might conjure vivid reminders of a popular past movie. We all need deliverance at some, or many, points in our lives.

GOD'S PLAN FOR FREEDOM

The Israelites desperately wanted to be delivered from Egypt. The story of their flight to freedom is recounted in Exodus 12:

> *During the night Pharaoh summoned Moses and Aaron and said, "Up! Leave my people, you and the Israelites! Go, worship the Lord as you have requested. Take your flocks and herds, as you have said, and go. And also bless me." The Egyptians urged the people to hurry and leave the country. "For otherwise," they said, "we will all die!" So the people took their dough before the yeast was added, and carried it on their shoulders in kneading troughs wrapped in clothing. The Israelites did as Moses instructed and asked the Egyptians for articles of silver and gold and for clothing. The Lord had made the Egyptians favorably disposed toward the people, and they gave them what they asked for; so they plundered the Egyptians* (Exodus 12:31-36).

As with His own people, the Israelites, God's plan for your life never involves bondage. His desire is always to provide you with freedom. John 8 says:

Jesus replied, "I tell you the truth, everyone who sins is a slave to sin. Now a slave has no permanent place in the family, but a son belongs to it forever. So if the Son sets you free, you will be free indeed" (John 8:34-36).

DESPERATELY SEEKING DELIVERANCE

Going back to the Book of Genesis and reading about Joseph provides background about how and why the Israelites were living in Egypt. Joseph had been sold into slavery, but because he has God's favor, he works his way up to second in command of the entire land. The book ends at the point where Joseph sends for 70 of his family members to come to Egypt. Israel is experiencing a great famine, so Joseph makes plans for his family by securing land and provisions for them.

The Book of Exodus begins 350 years later. Joseph has died. The Pharaoh that he had found favor with has also died. The new Pharaoh does not know how all the Jews ended up in Egypt and sees them as a great threat to his land. He issues an edict that all of the male Jewish children are to be killed. The edict motivates Moses' mother to protect her baby boy. You may be familiar with the story of how she places him in a basket and floats him down river. Moses is found by someone associated with the Pharaoh's family who promptly takes him back to the palace. Coincidentally, the woman hired to care for the baby is his actual mother (see Exod. 2). This is no ordinary baby. God has put his finger on this particular baby in order to raise him up as a deliverer for the Israelites from bondage.

It is clear that God has a plan for freeing His people even before they know they need one. The edict that Pharaoh intends to destroy the Jewish people becomes the very thing that brings them deliverance. It is the same for your life now. The very things that the enemy intends to use in your life to lock you in prison and keep you in bondage can be the very things that God uses to bring deliverance for you!

MOVING FROM CAPTIVITY TO FREEDOM

There are some important things to understand about the concept of deliverance if you want to move from captivity into freedom.

Focus on reversal, not rehearsal.

Only the Lord can take the mess in your life and turn it around. God can take any mess that you have created or any mess that the enemy has brought into your life and make beauty rise out of the ashes. God can break through any bondage, bringing great things into your life.

What happens, however, is that many people tend to focus on how they got to the point of bondage rather than how to escape. As a result, they end up spending their lives in captivity. This thought process makes them fall for one of the enemy's plans.

If you rehearse your past over and over, it prevents God from being able to reverse it. God can use divine reversals to change the mistakes that you have made or end the curses that might have been spoken over you. God is about shifting those things so that you move into the place where He always intended for you—the land of freedom. God wants you to live there, but you will never arrive at that destination if you continually rehearse your past in your mind.

We often do this through the words that we speak. Proverbs 18:21 says, *"The tongue has the power of life and death, and those who love it will eat its fruit."* There are people in the Body of Christ who don't realize that they are speaking word curses over their life, thereby constantly keeping themselves in prison. They say that they want to be free, but they do things that prevent them from moving into freedom. This includes speaking death and spouting poison from their mouths. Here is how we can reverse things rather than rehearse them;

1. *Edit your past.* The word *edit* means to cut and put words, pictures, and film together in such a way that it

provides specific and succinct intent. The Lord wants you to go through and find mistakes in your mind and, by the blood of Jesus and through the help of the Holy Spirit, edit the sections that you do not need to play over and over again in your head. Hit the delete button!

Reverse things rather than rehearse things.

2. *Experience the present.* What is God saying to you today? What does He want you to experience today? God is not some guy who has to go drag junk out of your closet. He has fresh work for you, fresh bread for you, and fresh provision for you every day of your life. The question: What is He doing for you in your life right now? How can you draw from the good and the bad in order to experience the present?

3. *Enhance your future.* Expect the best. Enhance your future by laying a foundation of expectation and faith by speaking the promises of God over your life.

Many people have settled for a lesser-than lifestyle. You may have grown comfortable in your captivity. However, God's plan never involves bondage. Now is the time to edit the past, experience the present, and enhance the future.

Rich's future couldn't be brighter! I smiled from ear to ear watching his 6-foot, 7-inch frame stack boxes that had been packed with Thanksgiving food. The people of The Refuge would soon be delivering 500 of them throughout the city, and Rich was thrilled to be doing his part. It was only three months earlier that I had visited him in detox, a giant of a man who had been beaten down by the giant of addiction. But that was the turning point, as God began to edit Rich's past so he could launch him into his destiny. And here was Rich on a Sunday afternoon, enjoying the present, and thankful that his newfound journey with the Lord led him to levels of freedom he never knew existed, and a future full of promise!

Allow God to fight on your behalf.

Moses returned to the Lord and said, "O Lord, why have You brought trouble upon this people? Is this why You sent me? Ever since I went to Pharaoh to speak in Your name, he has brought trouble upon this people, and You have not rescued your people at all" (Exodus 5:22-23).

The answer for Moses comes in Exodus 6:1:

Then the Lord said to Moses, "Now you will see what I will do to Pharaoh: Because of My mighty hand he will let them go; because of My mighty hand he will drive them out of his country" (Exodus 6:1).

God was there to act on behalf of Moses—it was not in Moses' authority or position to act. God let Moses know that it was not his staff or the way he spoke that was going to turn the heart of Pharaoh. God told Moses that He had his back. In the same way, we have to allow God to act on our behalf. There is a fine line between accepting responsibility for the things that we have done to put us in bondage and allowing God to take the authority for us. You cannot blame others for the fact that you are not perfect. None of us are up to that standard. The bottom line: You have to accept responsibility for the things that you have done

> We have to rely on Him to step in and fight our battles.

in your life while, at the same time, allowing God to do what He does best—act on your behalf, rescue you, and deliver you.

We can consult all the self-help aficionados on television and in books, but the fact is that none of us has enough self-discipline and self-will to move from bondage into freedom without God's will in our lives. If we did, then we would not need God. But we do need Him! We have to rely on Him to step in and fight our battles. After all, He has already told us that the battle is the Lord's. Consider what it says in Psalm 44:

> *It was not by their sword that they won the land, nor did their arm bring them victory; it was Your right hand, Your arm, and the light of Your face, for You loved them. You are my King and my God, who decrees victories for Jacob. Through You we push back our enemies; through Your name we trample our foes. I do not trust in my bow, my sword does not bring me victory* (Psalm 44:3-6).

David, who is speaking in this passage, is saying that, although he is a skilled warrior, he does not have enough ability to win this battle. Psalm 44:7 says, *"But you give us victory over our enemies, you put our adversaries to shame."* If your prison is depression or materialism, then it is God who gives you victory over those things or over anything else that represents bondage to you.

While His plan involves freedom for you, the challenge is that it will never come without a fight. There is always a price to pay. History shows that any conquest and any war always involved a conflict with an enemy who tried to keep the opponent from achieving freedom. Your enemy today wants to put you in prison. Likewise, Pharaoh was not quick to let the Israelites go. There had to be a series of plagues from God, acting on behalf of the Israelites, before Pharaoh would let them go.

Here is the great news: We serve a God who will always outlast the enemy. However, for Him to do this, you must allow God to act on your behalf. It is your faith that keeps God engaged in the battle for your freedom. If this is to truly be the Lord's battle, then you need to keep your trust and faith in Him. As long as you do that, He is engaged in fighting for your freedom.

> ## We need to be ready to move in a moment's notice.

During the night Pharaoh summoned Moses and Aaron and said, "Up! Leave my people, you and the Israelites! Go, worship the Lord as you have requested. Take your flocks and herds, as you have said, and go. And also bless me" (Exodus 12:31-32).

For 350 years, the Israelites had been in bondage and in slavery. All of a sudden, they are sent out of the country to their freedom.

Deliverance is both instantaneous and progressive. The Lord can orchestrate events resulting in release from bondage at any time. If you truly believe that God's plan for your life involves freedom, then the promise of the Lord is that He is your deliverer and that deliverance will come for you. That is why you must be ready for a moment of breakthrough. It could happen in the middle of the night; it may be during a weekend service; you could be driving down the road; you may be sitting at your desk; or you could be enjoying breakfast. However it reaches you, this breakthrough moment will arrive, and the Lord will move you into freedom.

Preparing for Deliverance

You may be asking yourself, *How do I prepare for that? How can I make sure that I am ready?* The answer is to focus on these three things:

1. Proclaim your freedom even while you are held captive.

Power comes from being vocal. When you come into agreement about who the Lord is and proclaim your freedom even while you are still in prison, it releases the hand of God to act on your behalf. While you are still a prisoner, you need to write your declaration of independence and allow it to be signed by the blood of Jesus. You can do this by declaring, according to the authority of the Word of God, any of the following that applies to you:

- "I am a free man."

- "I am a free woman."

- "I will not be a slave to depression any longer."

- "I am not going to be a slave to crack cocaine any longer."

- "I am not going to be a prisoner to materialism any longer."

For each of these examples, you can also add: "Here is my declaration of independence. I am proclaiming by faith that I have been set free."

> As it is written: "I have made you a father of many nations."
> He is our father in the sight of God, in whom he believed—
> the God who gives life to the dead and calls things that are
> not as though they were (Romans 4:17).

We are like Him whenever we proclaim our freedom while we are still in bondage. This concept is vividly expressed in Isaiah 61:

> The Spirit of the Sovereign Lord is on me, because the
> Lord has anointed me to preach good news to the poor.
> He has sent me to bind up the brokenhearted, to proclaim

freedom for the captives and release from darkness for the prisoners, to proclaim the year of the Lord's favor and the day of vengeance of our God, to comfort all who mourn, and provide for those who grieve in Zion—to bestow on them a crown of beauty instead of ashes, the oil of gladness instead of mourning, and a garment of praise instead of a spirit of despair. They will be called oaks of righteousness, a planting of the Lord for the display of His splendor (Isaiah 61:1-3).

When we proclaim our freedom—even during captivity—we are positioning ourselves within the Lord and coming into agreement about who He is in relation to ourselves and those around us.

This is also the prophecy of the coming Messiah. The Messiah proclaims freedom for those in captivity and liberty for those in bondage. By proclaiming that you agree with what He has said and with who He is, you are identifying with Him. This declaration brings victory, breakthrough, and freedom into your life. It moves you out of the realm of the natural where you are focused on your bondage and into the realm of the supernatural.

2. Prepare for the breakthrough.

You must prepare for freedom just as the Israelites did in Exodus 12:34: *"So the people took their dough before the yeast was added, and carried it on their shoulders in kneading troughs wrapped in clothing."* The Israelites were expecting breakthrough, so they were prepared in the middle of the night to grab their stuff and go. They were ready at a moment's notice. Like the Israelites, it is important that you make preparation for breakthrough so that you begin to think, speak, and act as though you are already free.

You can prepare by doing certain things. For example, you need to have a vision for your life, your marriage, your kids, and your career.

In addition, there also needs to be a provision, which involves preparation. You have to provide for the vision rather than sit around and hope that it happens. There is action required on your part to make it happen. The Israelites made sure that they had provision for their journey. They provided for their vision, which was: "We do not belong here. We do not belong in slavery. We serve a God who has made promises to us, and we want to move out of this place of captivity into a place of inheritance." That is what God wants to do in your life as well.

When the Israelites moved out of the place of bondage, the Bible says that they carried their belongings on their shoulders. When you gain freedom, it does not mean that you will never have to work again. The work just becomes different. Instead of carrying bricks for Pharaoh, they are carrying bread for their future. When you operate in bondage, there is a burden and a weight on your shoulders. However, when there is a provision from the Lord for freedom in your future, you do not mind carrying that weight on your shoulders. There is an easiness that comes with that because God has equipped you for the future. God has allowed you to walk in freedom.

The sad truth: Many people do not want to be set free. Some people in jail right now do not want to get out because they have grown comfortable with captivity. They have a routine in which someone else tells them when to go to bed and when to eat. Someone provides meals for them and they do not have to work to put a roof over their head. In reality, they do not have to be responsible. The thought of moving into freedom within society scares them because they would then have to rely on themselves for support and the ability to know when to do things. Unfortunately, there are people in the Body of Christ today who think the same way. They have grown so comfortable in their captivity that the thought of moving into freedom paralyzes them.

> Think, speak, and act as though you are already free.

These captives will be left behind by God because His plan always involves freedom. He works with those who are prepared to meet their breakthrough and their deliverance by His hand. Ask yourself, *Do you want to serve a pharaoh or do you want to serve a Father?* If you are content in your captivity, then you will serve a pharaoh the rest of your life. But if you believe that there is an inheritance for you, then you will allow yourself to surrender to a Father and you will begin serving Him.

3. You must plunder.

The Israelites did as Moses instructed and asked the Egyptians for articles of silver and gold and for clothing. The Lord had made the Egyptians favorably disposed toward the people, and they gave them what they asked for; so they plundered the Egyptians (Exodus 12:35-36).

Scripturally, you have the right to demand that the enemy pay back what he has stolen from you.

When God is moving you out of captivity and into a place of freedom, He gives you license to plunder from the enemy and take treasure from him that rightfully belongs to you. This is because the enemy hoards things for himself while you are held captive. This is his opportunity to take liberties with your stuff, your health, your relationships, your career, and your finances. Consequently, that is why you have approval to go to the camp of the enemy and reclaim everything that belongs to you.

You serve a God who is all about restoration. He does not want to rub it in your face and point out your mistakes or the things that you might have lost. Instead, God tells you to go and reclaim what rightfully belongs to you. The Bible emphasizes this right in Psalm 3:8: *"From the Lord comes deliverance. May Your blessing be on Your people. Selah."*

Remember:

The blessing of the Lord is not an addiction to crack cocaine.

The blessing of the Lord is not sleepless nights because you are plagued with insomnia.

The blessing of the Lord is not a battle with depression for the rest of your life.

The blessing of the Lord is not that you rehearse word curses because your family screwed up or because the enemy has convinced you that your life is a mess.

That is a lesser-than lifestyle and you should not accept it because God has so much more for you. Paul writes about this in Philippians:

> *Yes, and I will continue to rejoice, for I know that through your prayers and the help given by the Spirit of Jesus Christ, what has happened to me will turn out for my deliverance. I eagerly expect and hope that I will in no way be ashamed, but will have sufficient courage so that now as always Christ will be exalted in my body, whether by life or by death* (Philippians 1:19-20).

Remember, too, it is one thing to get out of prison but it is another thing to *stay out* of prison. There are a lot of people who get out of prison but they do not sustain their freedom. They end up right back in captivity. We want to make sure that we retain our freedom and deliverance that God has provided.

The pathway for your deliverance is set before you, and it is time to journey with the Lord to the land of freedom. Go for it! You were made for freedom!

Chapter 10

Roll out the Red Carpet—
A Journey of Excellence

He who consistently plans each day will journey
successfully through all of life's years.
—Drew Eric Whitman

ALL of us make our share of mistakes and blunders. Television even offers programs highlighting the slips, falls, mistakes, and embarrassing situations of people. We watch these shows and laugh partly because we can relate to what we see. No one is exempt! Making mistakes is one thing that we all have in common. However, mistakes that happen as a result of a half-hearted effort, laziness, or a poor attitude can damage us and others. These actions often bring reproach on the Kingdom of God. Excellence is important in your life and in the church because there are three things at stake:

1. The saving of souls

2. Your own spiritual growth

3. The preservation of culture

IN SEARCH OF EXCELLENCE, NOT PERFECTIONISM

First Kings 10 speaks about excellence:

> *When the queen of Sheba saw all the wisdom of Solomon and the palace he had built, the food on his table, the seating of his officials, the attending servants in their robes, his cupbearers, and the burnt offerings he made at the temple of the Lord, she was overwhelmed* (1 Kings 10:4-5).

The Message Bible states the same passage this way:

> *The queen of Sheba heard about Solomon and his connection with the Name of God. She came to put his reputation to the test by asking tough questions. She made a grand and showy entrance into Jerusalem—camels loaded with spices, a huge amount of gold, and precious gems. She came to Solomon and talked about all the things that she cared about, emptying her heart to him. Solomon answered everything she put to him—nothing stumped him. When the queen of Sheba experienced for herself Solomon's wisdom and saw with her own eyes the palace he had built, the meals that were served, the impressive array of court officials and sharply dressed waiters, the lavish crystal, and the elaborate worship extravagant with Whole-Burnt-Offerings at the steps leading up to The Temple of God, it took her breath away.* (1 Kings 10:4-5 The Message).

The New Living translation says it a different way:

> *When the Queen of Sheba realized how very wise Solomon was, and when she saw the palace that he had built, she was overwhelmed. She was also amazed at the food on the tables, the organization of his officials, and the splendid*

clothing, the cup bearers, and the burnt offerings Solomon made at the temple of the Lord (1 Kings 10:4-5 NLT).

Do you believe that the Bible holds truths for us today as well as advice and wisdom that we can use in our lives? It is important to understand some things about what excellence is *not* so that you can understand what excellence *is* in relation to your life's circumstances. It is also important to differentiate between excellence and perfectionism. A perfectionist is an unhealthy person who takes the inadequacies and the inner turmoil of their life to try and perfect their outer environment in order to mask their inner turmoil or problems. A perfectionist is never happy until things are perfect. The problem with that thinking: things are never perfect. Therefore, these types of people are never happy.

Perfectionism is a sickness. Excellence is a standard. Edwin Bliss said, "The pursuit of excellence is gratifying and healthy. The pursuit of perfection is frustrating, neurotic, and a terrible waste of time."

Applying God's Principles for Excellence

God's Word contains principles that we should apply in our lives while other ones are important to the church. There are also principles that are important to you as a spouse, mom or dad, student, business owner, or as one employed by somebody else. Consider and meditate on three concepts related to what excellence does.

1. Excellence propagates excellence.

The word *propagate* simply means to spread or to grow, produce, generate, multiply, develop, breed, or create. Therefore, excellence produces, creates, develops, grows, spreads, multiplies, and breeds excellence. First Kings 10:1-10 explains this concept further:

> Perfectionism is a sickness. Excellence is a standard.

When the queen of Sheba heard about the fame of Solomon and his relation to the name of the Lord, she came to test him with hard questions. Arriving at Jerusalem with a very great caravan—with camels carrying spices, large quantities of gold, and precious stones—she came to Solomon and talked with him about all that she had on her mind. Solomon answered all her questions; nothing was too hard for the king to explain to her. When the queen of Sheba saw all the wisdom of Solomon and the palace he had built, the food on his table, the seating of his officials, the attending servants in their robes, his cupbearers, and the burnt offerings he made at the temple of the Lord, she was overwhelmed. She said to the king, "The report I heard in my own country about your achievements and your wisdom is true. But I did not believe these things until I came and saw with my own eyes. Indeed, not even half was told me; in wisdom and wealth you have far exceeded the report I heard. How happy your men must be! How happy your officials, who continually stand before you and hear your wisdom! Praise be to the Lord your God, who has delighted in you and placed you on the throne of Israel. Because of the Lord's eternal love for Israel, he has made you king, to maintain justice and righteousness." And she gave the king 120 talents of gold, large quantities of spices, and precious stones. Never again were so many spices brought in as those the queen of Sheba gave to King Solomon (1 Kings 10:1-10).

Excellence is not about materialism. It does not involve how much stuff you own. Excellence does not equate to a certain amount of money.

It cannot be bought. Why? Because excellence is a condition of your heart and your spirit. It is tied to attitude. The Queen of Sheba represents excellence, and she comes all the way from Egypt to witness the excellence and wisdom of Solomon. The principle illustrated here is that excellence attracts excellence. If you go into a store where things are done with excellence or if you go into a restaurant or a fast food place where things are done with excellence, it makes you want to shop there or eat there again. However, it has nothing to do with having the fanciest building in town. What attracts you is how things are done.

Now I have some idiosyncrasies about fast-food restaurants. My standards are probably unrealistic and way too high, but I have this expectation that when I walk into a fast-food restaurant, the person behind the counter will greet me and not grunt at me. I want to be greeted in a friendly manner. I have an expectation as well that the people being paid to take my order and serve my food will act accordingly and not as if I am inconveniencing them.

Because of my standards and expectations, I spend a lot of time at Chick-fil-A rather than at other fast food restaurants because of the excellent service. This fast-food chain has an environment and atmosphere of excellence that starts at the corporate office in Atlanta and filters all the way down through the organization to the store owners, the general managers, and the employees. It is an attitude of the heart. It is about being served by people who look at you and greet you with a smile—no grunting. They are friendly and appear to be thankful that you are in their restaurant. It means a lot when a place is clean and the food is prepared well. They even have fresh flowers on the tables and stop by to give you freshly ground pepper. This is a perfect example of how excellence attracts excellence.

Another example is my recent experience taking our daughter to her first year away at college. As the resident assistant

> Excellence involves going above and beyond what people expect.

handed us the keys to check into her dorm room, I jokingly asked, "Now, are you ladies the ones who move all of our stuff in?" One of them replied in a rather serious tone, "No sir, but the student helpers out front wearing green shirts will help you move in." I thought she was kidding. I turned around and saw students in green "MOVER" tee-shirts. They were available to help unload our stuff from our vehicle and carry it to the room. That type of assistance defines excellence because it involves going above and beyond what people expect.

I have this weird idea about how the church and believers should set the standard of excellence so that people look to us for a certain standard of excellence rather than to the world. The world could learn a lot from the church and from you as a believer. Excellence produces, generates, grows, breeds, and multiplies excellence. Excellence in your life will attract excellence. The way that you live, speak, work, and the way that you approach different things in life will attract excellence to your life. If you are casual with your relationship with the Lord and if you do not approach your walk with the Lord with excellence, then do not expect a lot of growth during your spiritual journey. If there is no thought to your devotional life and no plan to pursue Him in a proactive way, then you also cannot expect a lot of growth. However, if you approach your journey with the Lord with excellence and the Lord knows that it is a priority for you, then you can expect growth.

Regardless of how bad your day or week, you can still say, "I'm going to give my best to the Lord today because I serve a God who is a God of excellence and I believe that He deserves excellence from me." John Gardner says, "The society that scorns excellence in plumbing because plumbing is a humble activity and tolerates shoddiness in philosophy because it is an exalted activity, will have neither good plumbing nor good philosophy. Neither its pipes nor its theories will hold water."[1]

We should do everything in life with excellence. Students should approach their education with excellence. Workers, laborers, and professionals should work with excellence. When you show up for work you should work as unto the Lord. You may say, "My company does not deserve excellence on my part and it doesn't matter if I fudge a little bit on this or that or on the expense report or what time I clocked in." This is a wrong attitude. You are representing the Lord on earth, and you should do everything as unto Him, with excellence. You should be the most dependable person on the job. You should be the most prompt and the most professional person in your workplace. Excellence propagates excellence.

2. Excellences produces a right spirit.

> *Praise be to the Lord your God, who has delighted in you and placed you on the throne of Israel. Because of the Lord's eternal love for Israel, He has made you king, to maintain justice and righteousness* (1 Kings 10:9).

There is not much information about the Queen of Sheba. All we know is that, in verse 1, she tests Solomon with hard questions; and after seeing the excellence of Solomon, her attention diverts from Solomon to the Lord. That is the impact of excellence. The saving of souls and your spiritual growth are both at stake. If we approach the things of life with excellence, then it will cultivate in us a right spirit.

> *Again, it will be like a man going on a journey, who called his servants and entrusted his property to them. To one he gave five talents of money, to another two talents, and to another one talent, each according to his ability. Then he went on his journey* (Matthew 25:14-15).

That word *ability* comes from the Greek word *dunamis*. That is the same word that we find in Acts 1:8 where it says, "*But you will receive power when the Holy Spirit comes on you; and you will be my witnesses in Jerusalem, and in all Judea and Samaria, and to the ends of the earth.*"

Dunamis is used in this Scripture in place of "power." That word literally means ability or an excellent spirit. It says that you will receive a right spirit or an excellent spirit after the Holy Spirit comes on you. Then you can be an authentic witness and a representation of Christ because you are reflecting the excellence of the Lord. Matthew 25 speaks about how excellence is an attitude of the heart. It is a teachable spirit; it is a servant's heart; and it is the heart of a person who is committed to excellence who says, "I want to serve and to learn new things so that I can have greater influence for the sake of the Kingdom."

What is interesting to note is that the root word for *excellence* in the Greek comes from the same word that means "to please." This makes the point that there is a strong link between spiritual excellence and a desire to please God. In Matthew 25, the owner entrusts his money to these men based on their excellence, based on their spirit, based on whether or not they have a servant's heart, a teachable spirit, or the heart of one who has excellence. He gives five talents to one man, two to another man, and one to the other based on their ability and based on their dunamis. The owner's reaction, after he returns from his journey, is the key. He discovers out that the one with five talents doubles it to ten, and the one with two now has four.

But the man with one talent did not have a servant's heart, a teachable spirit, or a spirit of excellence. He buries the talent in the ground and says, "I know you are a hard taskmaster so I buried it in the ground because I was afraid that, when you returned, I wouldn't have it." Notice the reaction of the master:

> *Take the talent from him and give it to the one who has the ten talents. For everyone who has will be given more, and he will have an abundance. Whoever does not have, even what he has will be taken from him* (Matthew 25:28-29).

The owner has this reaction because God rewards good stewardship and an excellent spirit with greater influence. In other words, if you illustrate that you are a good steward of the things that God has given you—you show yourself to be a person of excellence—then God will entrust more opportunities to you as well as greater resources, finances, influence, and relationships into your life.

John D. Rockefeller Jr. is widely recognized as having said that the secret to success was to do common things uncommonly well. While it is good to do something well one time, it is another thing to do good things on a repetitive basis. That is the difference between a standard and a system. Anybody can clean their room one time. If you do not have a system in place, then chaos will return within a couple of weeks or maybe within a couple of days, depending on how you live. If you do not have a system of excellence in your life or a system in your relationship with the Lord, your finances, your marriage, the way you raise your kids, or in your business, then you will find yourself digressing into the same old patterns. It is about being a steward of the Lord's talents. It is about producing a right spirit. It is about being a steward over the things that God puts in your hands so that He will entrust you with more for the benefit of His Kingdom.

3. Excellence prepares the atmosphere.

In Second Chronicles, Solomon begins building the temple. Prior to building it, he sends out a letter to Hiram, King of Tyre, and in that letter, Solomon says, "The temple that I am going to build will be great because our God is greater than all other gods." Solomon begins building the temple with excellence. This is one example of how Solomon builds with excellence:

> *The portico at the front of the temple was twenty cubits long across the width of the building and twenty cubits high. He overlaid the inside with pure gold. He paneled the main hall with pine and covered it with fine gold and decorated it with palm tree and chain designs. He adorned*

the temple with precious stones. And the gold he used was gold of Parvaim. He overlaid the ceiling beams, door-frames, walls and doors of the temple with gold, and he carved cherubim on the walls (2 Chronicles 3:4-7).

Notice the attention to detail. Again, excellence is not about material-ism nor is excellence defined by legalism. Legalism means adding stan-dards to the Word of God in order to make yourself acceptable to God. It might also involve attributing standards to someone else to make them acceptable to you. Excellence is a tool that is used to make God accept-able to humankind. It is not about us looking good nor does it relate to our reputation or how acceptable we are to God. Rather, it is about us making God personable and approachable to humankind. The saving of souls is at stake. Our spiritual growth is at stake, as well as the preserva-tion of a culture. We want to eliminate all distractions for ourselves and others. In other words, we do not want them to have to get past us to get to God. We serve a God who upholds a standard of excellence. Anything we do that is less than that is an improper reflection on the Lord. This idea is validated in Matthew 5:16: *"In the same way, let your light so shine before men, that they may see your good deeds and praise your Father in heaven."*

It is not a matter of whether your light is shining. If you have Christ inside you, then He is the light of the world and He will shine through you. It is a matter of *how* you let your light shine. Let your light *so* shine. The word *so* is an adjective and it describes the way that you let your light shine. Do you realize that you are God's advertisement here on earth and that people judge God based on your actions and attitude? That is why you maintain standards of excellence in every area of your life. There-fore, when you represent Christ, you should do it with excellence. Watch what happens as the result of excellence:

The priests then withdrew from the Holy Place. All the priests who were there had consecrated themselves, regardless of their divisions. All the Levites who were musicians—Asaph, Heman, Jeduthun and their sons and relatives—stood on the east side of the altar, dressed in fine linen and playing cymbals, harps and lyres. They were accompanied by 120 priests sounding trumpets. The trumpeters and singers joined in unison, as with one voice, to give praise and thanks to the Lord. Accompanied by trumpets, cymbals and other instruments, they raised their voices in praise to the Lord and sang: "He is good; His love endures forever." Then the temple of the Lord was filled with a cloud, and the priests could not perform their service because of the cloud, for the glory of the Lord filled the temple of God (2 Chronicles 5:11-14).

They did not just open it up and say, "Hey, anyone want to play the trumpet? Come on up, give it a try. We're going to dedicate the temple of the Lord. Come on, we're getting anybody we can up here." No, they rehearsed and prepared. They had the best singers and trumpeters that they could find because this was important. This was a temple built with excellence, and they wanted to dedicate it to an excellent God.

Why was the glory filling the temple of God? Because excellence prepares the atmosphere for the movement of God and for transformation.

The name Stradivarius is synonymous with fine violins. The reason: Antonius Stradivarius's philosophy was that he did not want a violin sold unless everything humanly possible had been done to perfect it. Antonius Stradivarius had a similar concept about God when he said, "God needs violins to send His music into the world. And if any violins are defective, God's music will be spoiled."[2]

Too many times, God's heart and God's expression to the world have been spoiled because the church and the people of

> Excellence prepares
> the atmosphere
> for the movement
> of God and for
> transformation.

God have not upheld a standard of excellence. People have said, "Oh, you know, if we don't have the best, it doesn't really matter. Let's just do the best we can and not really pay attention to the details." People have been distracted from the Lord as a result of our shoddiness, poor attention to details, and a lack of commitment to excellence.

There are three things at stake: the saving of souls, your own spiritual growth, and the preservation of a culture that passes down standards of excellence. I challenge you—as a business owner, worker, student, husband, wife, mom, dad, and believer—to recommit yourself to a standard of excellence. Your journey of life must involve a commitment to excellence.

ENDNOTES

1. http://www.mwboone.com/library/quotes2.php.
2. *Our Daily Bread* (Grand Rapids, MI: RBC Ministries, January 25, 1993).

Chapter 11

I'm All In—
A Journey of Expectation

"The hardest part of any journey is taking that first step."
—Anonymous

*E*XPECTATION is defined as a strong belief that something will happen or it will be the case in the future. Expectation is an interesting thing. Have you ever taken several big gulps from a glass, thinking that it was iced tea or soda and instead it was water or lemonade? Or maybe you expected water and the glass was actually clear soda? It's quite a jolt. All of a sudden, what you expected was something different.

Life can be that way as well. We begin a new job or enter school with a certain set of expectations. We approach a career, marriage, relationship, friendship, or church with a certain set of expectations and, sometimes, things happen that we don't expect. As a result, we find that life is full of disappointments. If we don't respond the right way to disappointments, then we may be severed from our destiny. Mishandled disappointments can cut us off from our appointed purpose in life. In other words, they will "dis-appoint" you from the destiny that God inscribed on our hearts.

That is almost what happens to the people in Joshua 3. They nearly allowed themselves to be separated from their destiny.

> So when the people broke camp to cross the Jordan, the priests carrying the ark of the covenant went ahead of them. Now the Jordan is at flood stage all during harvest. Yet as soon as the priests who carried the ark reached the Jordan and their feet touched the water's edge, the water from upstream stopped flowing. It piled up in a heap a great distance away, at a town called Adam in the vicinity of Zarethan, while the water flowing down to the Sea of the Arabah (the Salt Sea) was completely cut off. So the people crossed over opposite Jericho. The priests who carried the ark of the covenant of the Lord stood firm on dry ground in the middle of the Jordan, while all Israel passed by until the whole nation had completed the crossing on dry ground (Joshua 3:14-17).

The Israelites journey out of Egypt and spend 40 years wandering in the wilderness. It takes them years to get out of Egypt and it takes God years to get Egypt out of them. In the passage from Joshua, we find them just moments away from possessing their promise and from possessing their destiny. They are close to crossing their final barrier and moving into the land that God promised to give to them. That land represents their destiny and their inheritance. One final challenge of faith and obedience stands in their way.

We can never eliminate every disappointment from our lives. It would be great if, somehow, we could remove all of the disappointments or exempt ourselves from ever being disappointed again. However, if we follow some very simple instructions from the Israelites' journey, we can achieve two things. First, we can reduce our number of disappointments;

and second, we can elevate our level of expectation. There are three points from the story in Joshua that are applicable to our lives.

Submit and Obey

Early in the morning Joshua and all the Israelites set out from Shittim and went to the Jordan, where they camped before crossing over. After three days the officers went throughout the camp, giving orders to the people: "When you see the ark of the covenant of the Lord your God, and the priests, who are Levites, carrying it, you are to move out from your positions and follow it. Then you will know which way to go, since you have never been this way before. But keep a distance of about a thousand yards between you and the ark; do not go near it" (Joshua 3:1-4).

We serve a God who is fresh as well as full of creative ideas and opportunities for our lives. He never wants to see us stagnate in our relationship with Him. We serve a God who wants to lead us into new things. He desires to do new things in our lives and in our relationship with Him. There is a presence of God inside us that will lead us into new things if we are willing to go there.

Two elements that go hand in hand will make this happen—submission and obedience. Submission and obedience are the keys to moving into our destiny or into our Promised Land. It is possible to obey without being submissive. Some people even think obedience is enough. This is not the case. Both men and women have to be obedient and submissive. These are characteristics that God expects us to have in our lives in order to move into the promises of God.

If you are submissive to God but not to the godly authorities whom He has put in your life, then you are not fully submitted to God. Some people think, "I can just follow God and submit to God, but I don't have to do what my boss says. I don't have to submit to my pastor. I don't have to submit to my husband, or to other leaders that God has put in my life. I can just submit to God because I'm following the orders of God." If that is your mind-set, then you are deceiving yourself.

> *Everyone must submit himself to the governing authorities, for there is no authority except that which God has established. The authorities that exist have been established by God. Consequently, he who rebels against the authority is rebelling against what God has instituted, and those who do so will bring judgment on themselves* (Romans 13:1-2).

If you are submitting to God but have a rebellious spirit toward the authorities God has put in your life, then you are rebelling against God. That is a serious thing. Some young people think, "I can serve God, but I don't want to submit to my parents." When you are rebelling against your parents, you are rebelling against the Lord because they are the authority God has established in your life. If you rebel against your boss, the authority figure that God has established in your life, then you are rebelling against the Lord. If you rebel against those over you in school, in the community, or in the church, then you are rebelling against God. When you rebel against God, you damage your own spirit.

Obedience without submission is rooted in rebellion. Obedience that flows out of submission is rooted in devotion. There is a big difference. When you have obedience that flows out of submission, you recognize the authorities God has put in your life, and out of honor to the Lord you honor those authorities. Then you are willing to obey—not out of a rebellious, grit-my-teeth, "I've got to do this to please God" attitude—but out of devotion for the Lord, out of love for God, and out of

> When you rebel against God, you damage your own spirit.

passion for your heavenly Father. When you have submission and obedience as characteristics in your life, you have established divine order. When you have established divine order, you can expect the rest of your journey to be met with divine favor.

THEY CONSECRATED THEMSELVES

Joshua 3:5 says, *"Joshua told the people, 'Consecrate yourselves, for tomorrow the Lord will do amazing things among you.'"* To consecrate something simply means that you dedicate that or set it apart for a stated purpose. In the Scriptures, there are many things consecrated to the Lord. Two examples include Exodus 30:30: *"Anoint Aaron and his sons and consecrate them so they may serve Me as priests,"* and Leviticus 20:7: *"Consecrate yourselves and be holy, because I am the Lord your God."*

There are many other examples as well. In Leviticus 25, the fiftieth year is consecrated, dedicated, set apart for the purpose of God. In Leviticus 16, blood is consecrated. In First Samuel 21, bread is consecrated. In Judges 17, they consecrated silver, set it apart, and dedicated it for the purpose of God. Sons, altars, the temple, animals, and meat are all consecrated, dedicated, and set apart for the purposes of God. What is consecrated the most to the Lord in the Scriptures? People who dedicate their lives to making a difference for the cause of Christ.

God is still looking for people who will dedicate their lives, minds, work, dreams, money, stuff, kids, hands, mouths, and everything they have for the purpose of God. Acts 13 says that David served the purpose of God for his generation. In other words, David allowed himself to be dedicated for the purpose of God for his generation. David said that it is not about what he wants to do but what matters most is how he can make a difference for the Lord. When you consecrate your life for the Lord and decide that you are going to set your life apart for the purposes of God for this generation, you raise your level of expectation and will see amazing things that God will do in you. Submitting and obeying, as well as consecrating yourself in the Lord, are simple, yet effective, processes.

Follow the Presence of God

The Israelites followed the presence of God. Officers went through the camp giving out orders to the people. Then the people consecrated themselves and said something like, "We don't want to blow this. We can see our promise right across the river. Our destiny is right there. This is what we've waited years for, and we don't want to mess this up. So we're dedicating ourselves. We are presenting ourselves as living sacrifices. We are setting ourselves apart for the purposes and promises of God. And we are willing to follow His presence."

That was the order the officers gave, as stated in Joshua 3:3: *"...When you see the ark of the covenant of the Lord your God, and the priests, who are Levites, carrying it, you are to move out from your positions and follow it."* Verse 6 says, *"Joshua said to the priests, 'Take up the ark of the covenant and pass on ahead of the people.' So they took it up and went ahead of them."*

One of the keys in life is learning to put the presence of God out front. You must learn to follow the presence of God over your own whims, desires, and opinions of other people. If you have given your heart to Christ, then the person of the Holy Spirit lives inside of you. No longer is the presence of God housed in a box with angels on top carried on the shoulders of men, but God says you have now become the tabernacle of His presence. You become the carrier of the presence of God.

Let's not be flippant about this. The Almighty God of the universe has chosen to live on the inside of us. His presence is perfect and powerful. God allows His presence to be inside people like us. It is exciting to know that His presence is living inside of me. The presence of the Holy Spirit is very good and very faithful to lead us where we need to be. The issue is not with Him. The problem is that, oftentimes, we do not want to follow Him.

The Holy Spirit may say, "Get out of this relationship while you have the opportunity." And we say, "Oh, no, I kind of like it here." In response, the presence of God moves on and we stagnate. Or the Holy Spirit may say, "I know that they are offering you a job, but this is not what I have for you; I'm going to move somewhere else." Our response: "I'm tired of waiting, so I'm going to sign the deal." Oftentimes, we do not want to move with the presence of God. The presence of God is faithful in leading us where we need to be at the right time. Hence, following the presence of God is key to moving into our destiny and into our Promised Land. God wants to lead us by the Holy Spirit, but we have to be willing to follow Him even if it does not make sense.

What He says to you might not compute, or it might go against every bit of logic that is on the inside of you, but what is most important is that you follow the anointing of the Holy Spirit.

The Israelites decide to submit and obey; they are going to consecrate themselves; and they are going to follow the leading of the presence of the Holy Spirit. Because of that, they go from good to great. They go from good to God. That is what following the presence of God will do in your life. If you anchor expectations in the realm of the *horizontal* or in the realm of relationships, career, company, business, boss, husband, wife, or in a church, then you are guaranteed to experience disappointments.

However, if you anchor your expectations in the realm of the *vertical*, then you have moved from good to God. In the realm of the horizontal, there are many good opportunities. There are many good careers. There are many good schools, churches, husbands, and wives. There are good cities to enjoy. However, we must first choose to follow the presence of God, which will move us from good to God.

You must determine whether or not something represents a good opportunity or a God opportunity.

1. Is this a good job or is this a God job?

> Be willing to follow
> Him even if it does
> not make sense.

2.   Is this a good career or is this a God career?

3.   Is this a good spouse or is this a God spouse for me?

We need to know what the God things are in our lives, rather than just the good things. If we want to possess our land and possess our promise, then we have to go from good to God. The only way to make that happen is to follow the Holy Spirit's lead. Following His presence does not mean that you will eliminate every disappointment. We know that because, even while following the presence of the Lord, unfair things happen to righteous people. We know that those kinds of things go on in life. There will continue to be disappointments.

However, when you follow the leading of the Holy Spirit, you reduce the number of disappointments in your life and you raise the level of expectation. That is what the Israelites did—submitted and obeyed, consecrated themselves, and followed the presence of the Holy Spirit. Now maybe you think that because they did those things they could sit back and say, "Now, God, there's this one final barrier, one final obstacle, and we're going to sit here and wait until angels come from Heaven and construct a bridge so we can walk across to the Promised Land."

God rarely gives us that luxury. Occasionally God has allowed us to just sit back and wait for things to happen after we have submitted and obeyed and after we have consecrated ourselves, but most of the time, God requires that we engage our faith. Joshua 3:15 says that the Jordan River was at flood stage, but verse 13 tells us that they had great expectation. In fact, Joshua says that when the priests set their feet in the water, the waters would part and the Israelites would walk across on dry ground. That was expectation. They had to do something. They had to step in. They had to be proactive.

When the Jordan is at flood stage those three months out of the year, the water is too deep to wade in and see what God will do. They could not say, "We'll just ease into this idea and, if it doesn't work, we'll go back to the bridge idea." Stepping in at flood stage means they are all the way in. Many people in the Christian life and on their Christian journey want to play it safe. They sort of wade in and say, "I'm going to see what God will do. I've got some expectation but let's just see what the Lord is going to do here." But the Lord says, "No, we don't play that way. You are either in or you can hang out on the bank and miss your promise."

STEP IN

The Jordan is not some big, expansive river. It is fairly narrow even at flood stage. The Israelites could see the Promised Land from the opposite bank. You may be right there, too. You have taken the journey. You have walked through some stuff. You can see your promise. You can see your destiny. The Lord says there is one last step that you have to take. You are either in or you can spend the rest of your life on the banks of the Jordan. What are you expecting from God? Expectation is just a strong belief that something will happen or that it will occur in the future. So what are you expecting from God today? What are you trusting in or believing Him for? Step in and step forward toward fulfilling your expectation.

Here is an interesting truth. When the Israelites first came out of Egypt, one of the very first things that God did was part the waters of the Red Sea. Now here they are at the end of the journey 40 years later, and God is parting water again. This is God's way of saying, "I was with you in the beginning. I'm with you in the end. I'm the Alpha and the Omega. I'm the author of your faith and I am the completer of your faith. I made a way for you when you came out of Egypt, and I will make a way for you now to move into your Promise Land."

God is saying the same thing to you. It is time for you to jump in and expect a miracle!

Chapter 12

Conclusion:
The Ultimate Journey

A S I write this conclusion, I am on a journey. I am stuck on a packed regional jet heading to Florida with a screaming child sitting directly behind me, bottled water that tastes like it came from a swamp, and a seat that is about as comfortable as a park bench. Ah the joys of the journey!

The journeys of life are not all limos and luxury. The hardships and challenges along the way, at times, seem insurmountable. On the one hand, inconveniences, irritations, uncertainties, frustrations, and irritating people are all part of life. On the other hand, we experience thrills by the thousands, awesome victories, and those take-your-breath-away moments that keep us striving for all that life has to offer.

As already stated, some people get so focused on the destination that they miss great treasures along the way. By embracing all aspects of the journey, we learn about ourselves, others, and the characteristics that make life such a great adventure.

The journeys of life shape our lives for the present and, more importantly, for our future. Although it is important not to get so focused on the destination that we miss the journey itself, we cannot ignore the fact that each journey leads somewhere. Or, does it?

The ultimate journey for each of us is when we receive our boarding pass and travel from this life to the next. The interesting thing about it is that we do not get the privilege of booking the trip. Some people enjoy the journey of life for 70, 80, 90, or more years. Other people's journeys last only a decade or two or three.

The ultimate journey begins when you believe that there is life after death. Some think that upon death, we just cease to exist and there is nothing more. Some believe that people get another shot here on earth returning for round two as a horse, eagle, or other creature. If those who do not believe that there is eternal life in either Heaven or hell after death are right, then those who do believe have lived life under a false pretense. However, if there is life after death as well as a real Heaven and hell, what does that mean for those who do not believe?

All of this brings up another question for consideration. If there is a real Heaven and hell, what destination will be stamped on your ultimate journey boarding pass? Establishing a personal relationship with Christ—something much different from merely being religious—ensures your eternal heavenly destination.

The second of the Ten Commandments—often viewed by many as the ten suggestions—is that we are forbidden to worship idols. Idol worship conjures images in most people's minds of ancient Egyptians worshiping the figures of human bodies with animal faces or the Mayans donning grotesque masks and sacrificing other humans. Idols today are less tangible. However, idolatry still exists. We allow the pursuit of fame, fortune, influence, or material possessions to take the place of God in our lives. We dethrone Him and place self or things in His place on the throne of our hearts. Establishing a relationship with Him, or reestablishing one, requires a willful, conscious decision to dethrone self and to give the Lord authority in our lives.

We are living in times when so many things like the economy, employment, the stock market, leaders, political systems, and families are failing. The stability of many has been rocked, leaving thousands upon thousands wondering to what and to whom they can anchor their lives and their future. "Everything changes" is a concept captured by many lyricists in song. Nothing seems sacred or stable.

There is One, however, who never changes and is always stable. He is not wringing His hands in fear over the economy or over failed banks. He is not wondering how He is going to bail us out, and He is not on the verge of a breakdown or fit of rage. What is His name? Jesus! He is the same yesterday, today, and forever. You can anchor your life to Him and secure your ultimate journey in the future. It is as simple as dethroning yourself, trusting that His love for you is unconditional, and inviting Him to come into your life and be seated at the place of authority.

There is much traveling ahead—whether here in this life or afterward. So, grab your navigation tools, your map, and your spirit of adventure so that you can forge ahead. The journeys await you!

AUTHOR MINISTRY PAGE

For more information about Jay Stewart,
please visit www.TheRefuge.net.

You can also follow him on Twitter as Jay_Stewart.

ALL PROCEEDS FROM THE SALE OF THIS BOOK
GO TO TWO PURPOSES:

1. Helping rescue girls from the sex trafficking industry in Moldova

2. Providing fresh water and malaria prevention in Tanzania

Roadtrip Notes

Additional copies of this book and other book titles from DESTINY IMAGE are available at your local bookstore.

Call toll-free: 1-800-722-6774.

Send a request for a catalog to:

Destiny Image® Publishers, Inc.

P.O. Box 310
Shippensburg, PA 17257-0310

"Speaking to the Purposes of God for This Generation and for the Generations to Come."

**For a complete list of our titles,
visit us at www.destinyimage.com.**